We're from different generations; I'm older, Danita is younger. Our stories are different, yet the same. I lost my precious daughter to liver cancer while she lost her amazing husband in a climbing accident. Our pain hurts the same. In *When Mountains Crumble*, Danita is vulnerable and heart-wrenchingly honest, giving both practical help and spiritual wisdom gleaned during her walk through the Valley of Weeping. I highly recommend this book!

LINDA DILLOW, author of *Calm My Anxious Heart* and *Satisfy My Thirsty Soul*

This book sparkles with authenticity that acknowledges the angst of unanswered questions. It's also refreshing, creative, unique, and riveting. If you've lost a loved one or if you've been looking for the ideal resource to put into the hands of someone who is grieving due to death, or an unexpected crisis that has dramatically changed life's trajectory, buy this book. The author offers no quick fixes; instead, she provides support for the next step in the journey. *When Mountains Crumble* is a timeless treasure you'll want on hand to give to anyone who is experiencing loss.

CAROL KENT, speaker and author, *When I Lay My Isaac Down* and *He Holds My Hand*

When your world is rocked by the death of a loved one, the tumble of emotions and weight of decisions in the aftermath are overwhelming. In *When Mountains Crumble*, you will find a pathway through the labyrinth of grief so you can wrangle your emotions, find comfort in your sorrow, and find hope for your future.

ROBYN DYKSTRA, national Christian speaker; author of *The Widow Wore Pink*; two-time widow

When Mountains Crumble offers no sugar-coated shortcuts through the rocky terrain of sorrow. Drawing deeply from her own experience of loss and her daily reliance on the Holy Spirit, Danita Jenae provides a Scripture-sketched map for the twisting, turning journey of grieving and healing. Be prepared to weep, to laugh, and to roll up your sleeves for the hard, grace-filled work of grief. Because, as Danita reminds us, "No one fights alone."

JACK NEWMAN, American Bible Society

Dear one, are you going through grief? Has something tragic transpired to one you love and adore? Get this book. Now. Don't wait. Danita has woven a beautiful tapestry of comfort, gentle direction, and knowledgeable advice that will be your faithful companion on this journey of mourning.

SARAH PHILPOTT, author of *Loved Baby: 31 Devotions Helping You Grieve and Cherish Your Child after Pregnancy Loss*

Much like the beloved allegory *Hinds' Feet on High Places*, Danita has invited the reader into a transforming journey by the goodness and mercy of God. I was moved to tears more than once, not just because of her immeasurable heartache—rather, due to the powerful, poignant way she artistically wove God the Father, Jesus, and the Holy Spirit into everyday struggles. This book is a priceless friend in print, drawing the reader into their own story.

MARY JO PIERCE, intercessor, speaker, and author of *Adventures in Prayer* and *Follow Me: An Unending Conversation with God*

When Mountains Crumble is thought-provoking, honest, challenging, and outright good reading. As a widow, I readily identify with the fog, the shock, the sorrow, and even the dumb decisions she experienced. It helps a widow navigate through her grief by answering the personal questions posed and lets others better understand and pray for anyone who has experienced the loss of a loved one.

QUIN SHERRER, author of *Hope for a Widow's Heart*

Danita powerfully weaves grief and hope, sorrow and beauty, with a grace that invites us in and creates a space to be real with where we are in our loss. By not pretending, not burdening with pious formulas or "shoulds," this guide gives breath when it feels like we cannot breathe.

BISHOP KEN ROSS, Anglican Diocese of the Rocky Mountains

I wholeheartedly recommend *When Mountains Crumble* to all my GriefShare participants! Danita is truly a gifted writer. I love how honest and vulnerable she is with her own grieving, as well as the questions for self-reflection at the end of each chapter. I wish I could have had this resource when my husband died of a brain tumor.

DEBBIE BEATTY, hospice nurse, GriefShare coordinator, military widow

As a trauma-trained counselor, I have seen many walk the journey of grief, loss, and trauma. Danita has written a powerful, beautiful book, the perfect wise and gentle companion for anyone walking through grief. Offering a practical vulnerable peeking into her own grief story laced with Scripture and hope and a safe space to feel all the feelings—this is a treasure for those walking in deep darkness. This book is a seasoned guide, a refuge, and a journey toward step-by-step healing. I will be giving this book out to any client/friend going through grief.

JENNIFER HAND, Executive Director of Coming Alive Ministries; author of *My Yes Is on the Table: Moving from Fear to Faith*

Danita Jenae has written one of the most profound books I've ever read on grief! Authentic, passionate, and provocative, Danita gently leads the reader toward hope. I highly recommend!

BECKY HARLING, conference speaker and bestselling author of *How to Listen So People Will Talk* and *Psalms for the Anxious Heart*

After losing our son, a Lieutenant Colonel in the US Air Force, the grief was overwhelming. Danita has captured the journey through grief eloquently, lovingly, and truthfully. We highly recommend this book to anyone who has lost a loved one, or anyone who wants to understand how to love and encourage those who have.

PAUL AND ANITA, proud Gold Star parents

When Mountains Crumble tenderly places a powerful tool of hope into the hands of one lost in grief. Beautifully written with honesty and compassion, Danita shines a light on one of the darkest paths of human experience, giving voice to our fears as she shares her own story with courageous authenticity. This book is the perfect gift for someone grieving.

ERICA WIGGENHORN, author of *Letting God Be Enough: Why Striving Keeps You Stuck and How Surrender Sets You Free*

We all need a friend to talk to when life is hard. In *When Mountains Crumble*, Danita warmly invites readers into conversation, reflecting on grief together and making space for God's rebuilding work to begin.

CLARISSA MOLL, author and cohost of *Christianity Today's Surprised by Grief* podcast

How I wish I had these words to hold in my hands and heart after the loss of our two sweet babies. This grace-filled devotional reminds us we are not alone; we have a Savior who will carry us through the deep waters, leading us straight into His love.

CARLIE KERCHEVAL, author and cofounder of Marriage Legacy University

As a recent widow and still very fresh in my grief, this beautiful balm of a book is so soothing to my sad and hurting heart. Danita's writing is filled with a raw honesty—the kind that makes you nod your head without realizing it—and she blends in wisdom with a touch of humor that is so badly needed when in the midst of grief.

TRICIA MARCHAND, young widow and mom of two

I lost my first husband at twenty-three and my second at thirty-one years young. If only there had been this kind of hope written down for me! Danita's book is certainly helping demolish the mountain of aloneness in pain and grief for the widow. These devotionals will paint the words He wishes any young widow to know: I AM HERE.

RACHEL FAULKNER BROWN, director of Be Still Ministries and Never Alone Widows

Danita Jenae invites the grieving reader in, to wrestle, wade, and walk through their own loss of a loved one. Be comforted as you read truth from the Bible, journal, and experience healing to discover His strength to face your day!

DARLENE LARSON, author, Life Purpose Coach®, Grief-Loss Coach, Recovery Coach, founder of Hearts with a Purpose

Unfortunately, I've lost friends in all branches of the military, and recently lost my father, a Vietnam Veteran Marine, and have learned I can do much to heal by learning from others and trusting in God's unfailing love. In *When Mountains Crumble*, Danita has done a wonderful job presenting practical ways to help anyone experiencing grief rebuild by explaining much about what grief is and isn't, letting them know some of what to expect, and using devotional stories about her personal experiences with examples and questions to help guide those experiencing loss move forward with God's unshakable peace and unconditional compassion.

JOE LEWIS, USAF, Lt. Col. (Ret.); founder and CEO, Angels of America's Fallen

You never expect grief—even if you know it's coming. Danita takes your hand through the early days of loss, showing you that even though mountains crumble, God does not. This book is a much-needed companion on the grief journey.

TAMI IMLAY, military widow and mom; podcast host of *Her Restored Spirit*; Restoration Coach

After losing my mom, I have now read *When Mountains Crumble* three times; I still cry and laugh out loud many times throughout. God is going to bless so many through this book!

SARAH, headmaster and award-winning school teacher

Danita Jenae's words have been like a friend who understands, a balm. I can't wait to share the grief-birthed wisdom she's penned here with others. Danita has tossed out convention and in its place shares tested comfort about loving well to the end and about more than just-getting-by with God at our side.

RACHEL VIRGINIA, law enforcement widow

Because Danita was in a new community without a support network, she walked through the valley of the shadow of death leaning on Jesus. She will hold your hand through the valley with vulnerability. No religious platitudes or "should'ves" here. She shares transparent emotions, pain, courage, and hope.

TERRI BROWN, The Table Church

Danita Jenae is a woman on a mission to comfort God's people in lovingkindness. As a military missionary and seasoned military spouse, I have found that grief is all too often a large part of our shared story. This book speaks directly to women in pain, shepherding their hearts back to the One and only who can offer hope and healing.

MEGAN B. BROWN, author of *Summoned: Answering a Call to the Impossible*

I appreciate the realness of this book. As a widower myself, I can identify with so many things that Danita expresses in this book. Also the practical advice and the helpful insights are priceless. This will be a valuable resource in my counseling ministry!

CHRIS CARTER, Executive Director, Carter's Biblical Counseling, Widower

In this devotional guide, Danita Jenae's wrestling with God's truth and her experience is deeply real, and her openness is rare. I am confident this guide will help you know you are not alone, or crazy. It's like a friend who will help you sort through emotions, thoughts, and questions of "Where is God in all of this?"

TOM COFFAN, full-time Minister to Students for more than fifty years in Colorado

Danita speaks from a deeply authentic place, and I stand in witness to the work of God in her life while she traverses the tragic loss of her husband. I am excited for all the ways God will reach and encourage other people journeying through grief through this beautiful book.

ERIKA BLANKENSHIP, military spouse

Through this book, Danita passionately and practically helps others who have suffered the loss of a loved one. She is transparent, relatable, and honest; you'll no longer feel alone. Dan would be so proud of what Danita has done and I am too.

JANE DAVIS, Intercessory Prayer at Generations United Church, Niceville, FL

This book is a gentle powerhouse, not only because of Danita's poignant reflections but through the journal questions that help us process loss while pointing us to God's faithful and tender compassion.

LISA APPELO, sudden widow and single mom to seven children; author, *Life Can Be Good Again: Putting Your World Back Together After It All Falls Apart*

DANITA JENAE

WHEN MOUNTAINS CRUMBLE

REBUILDING YOUR LIFE

AFTER LOSING SOMEONE YOU LOVE

MOODY PUBLISHERS
CHICAGO

© 2022 by
DANITA JENAE

All Scripture quotations, unless otherwise indicated, are taken from the Holy Bible, New International Version®, NIV®. Copyright © 1973, 1978, 1984, 2011 by Biblica, Inc.™ Used by permission of Zondervan. All rights reserved worldwide. www.zondervan.com The "NIV" and "New International Version" are trademarks registered in the United States Patent and Trademark Office by Biblica, Inc.™

Scripture quotations marked ESV are from the ESV® Bible (The Holy Bible, English Standard Version®), copyright © 2001 by Crossway, a publishing ministry of Good News Publishers. Used by permission. All rights reserved.

Scripture quotations marked NKJV are taken from the New King James Version. Copyright © 1982 by Thomas Nelson. Used by permission. All rights reserved.

Scripture quotations marked KJV are taken from the King James Version.

Scripture quotations marked MSG are taken from THE MESSAGE, copyright © 1993, 2002, 2018 by Eugene H. Peterson. Used by permission of NavPress. All rights reserved. Represented by Tyndale House Publishers, a Division of Tyndale House Ministries.

Scripture quotations marked NLT are taken from the Holy Bible, New Living Translation, copyright ©1996, 2004, 2015 by Tyndale House Foundation. Used by permission of Tyndale House Publishers, a Division of Tyndale House Ministries, Carol Stream, Illinois 60188. All rights reserved.

Scripture quotations marked TLB are taken from The Living Bible copyright © 1971. Used by permission of Tyndale House Publishers, Inc., Wheaton, Illinois 60189. All rights reserved.

Scripture quotations marked ERV are taken from the Holy Bible: Easy-to-Read Version (ERV), International Edition © 2013, 2016 by Bible League International and used by permission.

All emphasis in Scripture has been added.

Names and details of some stories have been changed to protect the privacy of individuals. Any resemblance to persons known is purely coincidental.

Published in association with the literary agency of The Blythe Daniel Agency, Inc., P.O. Box 64197, Colorado Springs, CO 80962-4197.

Edited by Amanda Cleary Eastep
Cover design and illustration: Kaylee Dunn
Interior design: Erik M. Peterson
Interior illustrations: Danita Jenae
Interior calligraphy: Julia Deese

ISBN: 978-0-8024-2556-0

Originally delivered by fleets of horse-drawn wagons, the affordable paperbacks from D. L. Moody's publishing house resourced the church and served everyday people. Now, after more than 125 years of publishing and ministry, Moody Publishers' mission remains the same—even if our delivery systems have changed a bit. For more information on other books (and resources) created from a biblical perspective, go to www.moodypublishers.com or write to:

Moody Publishers
820 N. LaSalle Boulevard
Chicago, IL 60610

1 3 5 7 9 10 8 6 4 2

Printed in the United States of America

Dedicated to my Redeemer,
who can turn ashes into beauty and fertilizer into fruit.

In loving memory of my sweetheart, Dan,
and his legacy of strength and honor.

For our chickadees,
"Be filled with the peace and the love
and the joy of the Lord today."

CONTENTS

When Jesus began His ministry, He stood up and read a portion from this prophecy in Isaiah:

"The Spirit of the Sovereign LORD is on me,
because the LORD has anointed me
to proclaim good news to the poor.
He has sent me to bind up the brokenhearted,
to proclaim freedom for the captives
and release from darkness for the prisoners,
to proclaim the year of the LORD's favor
and the day of vengeance of our God,
to comfort all who mourn,
and provide for those who grieve in Zion—
to bestow on them a crown of beauty
instead of ashes,
the oil of joy
instead of mourning,
and a garment of praise
instead of a spirit of despair.
They will be called oaks of righteousness,
a planting of the LORD
for the display of his splendor.
They will rebuild the ancient ruins
and restore the places long devastated;
they will renew the ruined cities
that have been devastated for generations."

ISAIAH 61:1–4

Then Jesus rolled up the scroll and sat down, explaining: "While you heard me reading these words just now, they were coming true!"[1]

My Story and the
Sangre de Cristo Mountains

"Though the mountains be shaken
and the hills be removed,
Yet my unfailing love for you will not be shaken
nor my covenant of peace be removed,"
says the LORD, who has compassion on you.
ISAIAH 54:10

What do you do when everything you depend on falls apart? Where do you turn when your security collapses? When mountains crumble . . . then what?

For my family and me, the crumbling was both literal and figurative. I'm not sure how you lost your beloved, but when the one you depend on as your rock and stability dies, the devastation sounds a lot like, "No! No! No! This can't be happening. Mountains don't crumble!"

Even though I held on to that promise of unshakable peace and unfailing love in Isaiah 54:10, I also wrestled with it. It was hard to trust God's love wasn't failing me when everything else was failing me. It was hard to trust God's stability when everything else was falling apart.

After years of chronic autoimmune disease, insomnia, and postpartum depression, my husband and I didn't think I would pull through. Battling for my life taught us to fast, pray, and weep together. We learned to operate in heaven on earth. God healed me, and I felt whole for the first time in my life.

Shortly after that miracle, my husband Dan and I navigated our final military move back to the Colorado mountains where we first met and then married. We had one year left until his retirement and big dreams that were finally coming true. Everyone told us this would be our long-awaited season of rest. We believed that with all of our hearts.

Dan always came alive the minute we crossed over the state line to Colorado on our vacations and especially when we moved back. That big grin wouldn't leave his face, even when the mountains were not yet in sight. He met with the Lord best on the mountain. An adventurer and meticulous planner, Dan set a goal to hike all fifty-three of Colorado's "fourteeners" (mountains over 14,000 feet high). I loved his company, so it was hard for me to let him go on all those hikes until I saw how much they refueled his heart. He always returned to us with renewed compassion and love for us and for life.

The month after we moved back, Dan and I went hiking with our little girls. Cactus blossomed and wildflowers splattered joy over the desert canvas. I'd never seen anything like it in the rocky terrain of Colorado. After years of physical frailty, suffering, and illness, I was amazed that I could finally say to my husband, "Honey, I'm ALIVE! And I am HIKING with you!"

I got my life back right before Dan lost his. Grief on the heels of joy.

For over a decade of travels and intense responsibilities with the military, my prayer for my husband had been that God would *hide* and *cover* him in the blood of Christ. He went *missing* and *died* in a mountain range that translates to "the blood of Christ," the Sangre de Cristos. This feels both tragically ironic and piercingly redemptive.

Dan was more like Jesus than anyone I've ever known. A kind and gentle leader who loved in self-sacrificing ways every day. He served widows in practical ways; he spiritually adopted many fatherless into our home and family. Dan was also full of adventure and full of life. He made us all feel seen. Dan wasn't perfect, but he knew how to say, "I'm sorry." He knew how to love unconditionally and forgive limitlessly. (I gave him lots of practice!) Everyone who knew him learned to be a better father and husband by watching how he cared for, prayed for, and loved our children and me. He was our cornerstone and rock. He was our everything. And in a heartbeat, he was gone.

This is where the religious people want to interrupt and correct me. They say things like, "No. *Jesus* is your rock. *Jesus* is your stability." Well, of course He is. But this side of heaven, we depended on Dan. People try, but they just can't fix my grief by throwing Jesus into the hole Dan left. (Please don't do that to me or yourself or anyone else.)

Jesus didn't do that when Mary and Martha's brother died. He didn't preach at them or tell them it could've been worse. He didn't tell them to look on the bright side either. Instead, Jesus entered in, felt what they felt, and wept *with* them.[1] I wonder if all we really need in sorrow is someone brave enough, safe enough, and merciful enough to weep with us. It's hard to find friends like that.

This tragedy hit our family while we were still house hunting, and the move compounded the loss. My daughters and I had no home, no church, no friends, and no community. And with no warning, no husband and no daddy either. Our promises of rest weren't fulfilled; our big dreams didn't come true. And I was left with empty arms, an aching heart, and fistfuls of insufferable questions.

In the depths of this isolation, with no one to comfort me, I found one who never left my side, who asked me helpful questions when I was ready to process, and who sat quietly when I didn't want to talk. These are names of God that I would not know so intimately if it weren't for all the suffering and heartache—*Wonderful Counselor, Shepherd, Friend.*

I found I needed Jesus more than ever, but I also needed His people more than ever. (What a vulnerable position to be in.)

I'm deeply grateful for the sacrificial support of my parents and Dan's parents. And I'm thankful for the people who popped in and out of my story at just the right time like angels offering hot bread and respite. But often, I still felt alone and misunderstood.

By grace, I eventually stumbled onto the path with a few fellow companions in sorrow: some in the thick of loss like me (like Sam, who we call "Samwise," a brother in Christ who understands the ministry of presence) and some a few years ahead (like Rosalinda, a sister in Christ and widow with wisdom dripping from her fingertips). Long-distance prayer partners and old friends, like Tori and Erika, faithful and true, also helped shoulder the emotional weight and prayers. Each of them sat with me through day-long military briefings or a day or two at the social security office. Maybe that's all you need to know about their uncommon kindness and loyalty.

My companions asked me honest questions and gave me freedom to process those devastating, disorienting first months and years. They weren't trained counselors. But they were good friends who ushered me into the presence of the Wonderful Counselor.

If you'll allow it, this book will serve as your companion in sorrow. It can't replace counseling or grief support groups. But until you can even get there, I want you to know, deep within your soul, that you are not alone.

The Path to Peace

Sorrow has to run its course through us. In loss, we can't be fixed, rescued, or saved. Nor do we want to be. Sometimes, we just need someone to sit with us in the silence. Other times, we need to talk or write it out. That's when this book will be here for you—to offer words to pray when you feel like you can't pray and to offer a safe place to process your loss and your hope for what's ahead.

We'll begin with surveying the wreckage, acknowledging the ways our bodies and minds feel broken after loss. From there, we'll begin to lay foundations of spiritual practices that will help you to rebuild. We'll discuss practical ways you can rebuild your heart, your community, and your trust in God. We'll wrestle with your questions, doubts, regrets, emotions, and faith. In the end, prayerfully, this companion guide will lead you toward God's unfailing love and unshakable peace.

Revelation promises that this is exactly how we will overcome—by the blood of the Lamb and the word of our testimony.[2] Therefore, together, we will lean on two mighty themes for stability: the blood of Jesus and the power of telling your story. This interactive journey will help you find the words to honor your heart and the courage to tell your story.

When Mountains Crumble is a series of **devotional teaching stories**. After each story, you'll find **questions and creative prompts**. (These are not afterthoughts.) The questions of sorrow are the heart and soul of this book. Your answers (and noticing how they change over time) will become mile markers on the path of rebuilding your life after losing someone you love. Your answers will help you tell your story, which has healing power—first for yourself and then for those who hear it. Each devotional will end with a **prayer and Scripture references**. Because it's hard to do simple tasks in grief, we've put every devotional's

Scripture references in one printable, "The Scripture Sidekick." Print this out and cling to it because His Word is a healing balm and a lifeline for your journey ahead. You can find your Scripture Sidekick along with more of my story, free downloadable original artwork, and other resources at **companioninsorrow.com**.

Like our Savior, you and I are also well-acquainted with sorrow and its peculiar presence on the heels of joy. Thankfully, we know that Jesus will have the final say one fine day. But it seems the path to that day is through the Valley of the Shadow of Death. And I don't know about you, but I don't want to walk that road alone.

Walk with me?

Hanita jenae

———— ◆ ————

Dear Lord,

When we're met with sorrow, You promise to meet us with Your unfailing love, Your unshakable peace, and Your unconditional compassion. When our world crumbles, and we're slammed even lower than rock bottom, help us trust that there is a Rock of Salvation deeper still, and there is a Rock higher than us too. Help us begin to experience this truth: that You are our Rock, our Comforter, our constant source of stability. In Jesus' name, amen.

Grief 101

If you're exhausted and storm-tossed today, here's a quick crash course to help you find your footing.

Grief has only one expert.

The truth is, I'm no expert in your grief. No one can be an expert in your grief but you.[1] You'll find plenty of well-trained people who can help you, but no one can tell you what your grief "should" look like or feel like. Your loss is beautifully, painfully, and uniquely yours. But that's actually good news that comes with freedom to grieve in your own way.

Grief can feel isolating when it seems like no one gets you anymore. None but Jesus. It can feel even more isolating when your experience of loss doesn't line up with other people's experiences, expertise, or timelines. However, when we give each other freedom to grieve in our own unique ways, then we can actually comfort each other in a more authentic, helpful way. That said, I'm here because I'm hurting like you are. And I don't want you to feel as alone as I have.

"Grief work" is truly work.

As weird as it sounds, some find it helpful to schedule time to actively grieve. Maybe fifteen minutes each morning or an hour each weekend. That's a good time to sort through your memories or work through the journaling sections in this book. If you're the type who wants to grieve all the day long, a general cut-off time reminds you to take a break, regroup, and live again. If you can't find time to grieve, scheduling gives you permission to do so.

Grief work has no report card.

Why do people sometimes so easily shame, judge, and criticize the bereaved? I'm sorry if that's happened to you. People want us to assess and evaluate our grief: "How are you grieving?" Grief is not so clinical. This leaves us wondering, "Am I grieving the wrong way?" The big emotions you feel are natural, needed, and normal.

Grief has no formula.

While there is no step-by-step process to make our grief disappear (I know that's disappointing), there is a pathway through the valley that leads to life again. Discovering a hand to hold and ways to care for your soul will help you navigate these uncharted territories with more security and confidence.

Grief is not linear.

Grief can feel dizzying because it circles back around often. While I've been healed, I'm also still being healed. For that reason, you'll notice that this book doesn't follow the chronological order of my story. Instead, it follows an intentional, redemptive path toward your healing. Grief blurs time into "before death" and "after death," anyway. And what felt healed yesterday can suddenly feel cracked open today. Grief is not linear, but it does circle and re-circle closer toward healing. In the unfolding of these pages, my prayer is that you come to see and appreciate this cyclical nature as dark and beautiful poetry.

Grief is not depression.

There's a common misnomer that depression is one of the "stages" of grief. Sure, symptoms of depression sound akin to natural grief responses: feeling sad and hopeless; aching all over; gaining or losing weight; losing interest in activities; feeling guilty, angry, exhausted; lacking concentration. Sure, loss can set off depression. But don't assume grief equals depression. Grief and depression are clinically different things and need to be addressed accordingly.

Grief is not trauma.

I wish I realized sooner that my children and I were not suffering from only grief. Instead, we suffered from grief compounded with trauma. Hopefully, briefly bringing awareness here steers you in the right direction to seek adequate help. Some symptoms of Post-Traumatic Stress Disorder (PTSD) are uncontrollable flashbacks, nightmares, difficulty sleeping, high anxiety or fear, high alert, irritability, avoidance of triggering people/places/things, withdrawal, and developmental regression.

Often, the grief process feels stunted or paused until we heal from some trauma first. And that's okay. It's where we are at, and it's the body and mind's way of protecting us from processing too much at once. While PTSD is real, so is Post-Traumatic Growth. There is hope. Trauma doesn't have to define or trigger us our whole lives; healing is available.

Grief work has no deadlines.

Your timeline is only yours. It's a trap to expect to "get over it" by a certain date or time. And it's a trap to compare your healing journey and timeline with another's. Your loss, relationship, anointings, personality, and story are a million ways different than theirs. Therefore, our journeys are incomparable. So, don't compare them. There will be a day (or series of days) when the heaviness lifts, but you don't usually get to know any timestamps ahead of time.

Grieving has safe boundaries.

Some coping methods are healthier than others. But coping is still coping, and that's to be applauded if you ask me. Ask God to give you healthy coping strategies. If your grief work isn't destructive to yourself or others, then it's all fair in love and sorrow. The boundary line around grief is love. If we step out of love, then we're out of bounds. Even anger that doesn't hurt others is within the bounds of love. It's a healthy emotion that Jesus Himself feels too.

Loss can trigger destructive behaviors, causing harm to you or those around you. Behavior such as verbal or physical abuse, drugs or alcohol abuse, self-harm, cutting, or suicidal thoughts are outside the bounds of love. There's no shame and only freedom to be had in pursuing help from a qualified, grace-filled professional. The worst thing you can do is not tell anyone. Find someone safe to talk and pray with. You don't have to walk this alone.*

Grief is getting comfortable saying, "I don't know."

Understanding what grief is *not* helps us put healthy boundaries around ourselves. However, the difficulty is that all the big emotions and crazy thoughts within these boundaries have free reign. Trying to contain them feels like chasing chickens on a fifteen-acre fenced yard. I suppose you and I have our whole lives to decide

---

*National Suicide Prevention Lifeline: 1-800-273-8255 | TAPS Helpline: 1-800-959-TAPS (8277) For a prayer against hopelessness and suicidal thoughts, turn to the devotional, "when you want to give up."

what grief is. And what we decide will likely change over time.

I'm acutely aware that in a year or two, I may come back to this book and totally disagree with myself. Isn't that why we love *A Grief Observed*,[2] written by C. S. Lewis after his wife died? He makes firm declarations about loss in one chapter and revokes what he just said a few paragraphs later. That's just part of the territory.

Grief leaves us not knowing a lot of things that we used to feel certain about. After Dan died, my widowed friend, Rosalinda, asked me about a big decision I needed to make. My reply? "I don't know." She assured me, "There will be lots of 'I don't knows.' And that's okay."

I found we need to give room for the uncertainty and the questions to breathe. "Why?" seems to be a central question we'd all like to know the answer to, and yet, voicing our honest whys out loud feels hushed in grief culture. As if we should pretend we already accept that this is how it is. Why is this? I don't know.

This book was birthed out of all the "I don't knows" I was left with after losing someone I deeply love. I gave my questions permission to roam. Sometimes, I tried to wrestle them for an answer. Other times, I found great worth in simply acknowledging their existence in the room with me. *Why is this happening? Will I survive this? Can I go on? Who am I becoming now? Will any good come of it?* I don't know. I don't know. Is that Grief 101? That I may never get answers to my biggest questions? I'm not really sure. I don't know.

Grief is both honoring and honorable.

Something else I'm not really sure of is how my husband died. Sometimes, I feel like people want to know how someone died as a way of assessing value. My friends and I have lost loved ones for many reasons: car accidents, cancer, PTSD and suicide, drug overdose, divorce, murder, miscarriage. When in their prime or in old age, when overseas or state-side, in the air or on the ground, in a battle or in a bed. I'm here to say that no matter how your loved one died, and no matter how long they lived, their life and legacy have great value. When I think of loved ones I've lost, I rarely think of how they died. I think of *how they lived.* And I think of *how they loved.* Grieving is an honorable demonstration of your love. No matter how you lost your person, I honor your loved one, and I honor you for loving them.

Grief is becoming.

Like I said, there's a lot I don't know. But one thing I do know (now anyway) is that grief is a gift of becoming. Loss breaks us and reshapes us. And certain mysteries and revelations can only be plumbed in the Valley of the Shadow. We'll discover glimmers of wonder tilled into the soil of our sorrow as we walk this road together. You won't have to go alone.

For additional practical support, music playlists, Scripture cards, and printable artwork, grab your complimentary Grief Guide at **companioninsorrow.com**.

If you're not actively grieving yourself, but you're here because you want to know how to support your grieving friend or loved one, bless you and thank you! Your presence brings more comfort than you can imagine. You'll find resources just for you at **companioninsorrow.com**.

PART ONE

FOG AND SHOCK

(how grief affects you)

misplacing wednesdays
(grief brain)

"Sorrow makes us all children again,
destroys all differences of intellect.
The wisest know nothing."

RALPH WALDO EMERSON[1]

She didn't seem to understand why I presented myself in her office. With a lilt, I mumbled, "I'm Danita. I have a 10:30 a.m. appointment?" She informed me that our appointment was on Wednesday, which was yesterday. *Not again.* The bad news was I arrived twenty-four hours late. The miracle was I arrived fifteen minutes early.

Braving Wal-Mart was another miracle.

The first time I braved shopping at the superstore after Dan died, I wasn't prepared to pass the camping section, the automotive section, nor the peanut butter cups. Everything is and was Dan and his love and his absence.

I still cannot keep a single number in my head since Dan died. Can't remember my rent or utilities or other numbers one should keep. At the checkout line, I learned I cannot count to three either. And that's okay.

My four-year-old and I made it through checkout in a daze, yet triumphant. But when we arrived in the parking lot, I couldn't find my car anywhere. We were already exhausted from walking the aisles indoors, and here we were doing it all over again outside.

Is it okay to crumble to the asphalt and bawl in the middle of a Wal-Mart parking lot? I didn't think so either. A family drove by, telling me to use my car alarm beeper. "Can't, key battery is dead." A kid told me I really should remember where I leave my car. I had no words. *I can't. My husband is dead.*

I've burned more chicken since Dan died than in my entire life combined. I began to stutter and spell words backwards. I brushed my teeth with a tube of lotion. I schmeared the deodorant tube across my cheeks and forehead, mistaking it for my face stick. During the initial grocery-panic of the pandemic, when hot dogs were national delicacies, I left bulk quantities of milk, chicken tikka masala, and hot dogs out overnight.

This is referred to as "grief brain." My friend Rosalinda told me all about it.

I'm thankful for "prego brain" and "mommy brain" because they helped me understand grief brain. With mommy brain, the mind and body work double-time to process creating new life. With grief brain, we work double-time to process the death of life. In either case, you may feel like you have lost your mind. You have not.

You have a *fully* functioning mind. Your emotional swings, your forgetfulness, your moments of precise clarity and moments of complete illogical-arity . . . surprisingly, these are proof that your mind is working. Rosalinda told me this is good.

Your mind is working harder than it's ever worked before to process *what just happened.* It's working overtime to make sense of what doesn't make sense. Because we were never created for death. That wasn't part of the original plan. We were created for a life that never ends, to be loved endlessly.

Instead of being hard on your amazingly powerful mind, give

yourself excessive amounts of grace. The shaming or condemning thoughts that say: *You can't do this; it's too hard; you won't make it; see how dumb that was* . . . No. Tell them to be silent in the name of Jesus.

And your best defense after that?

Laughter. If given the choice to laugh or have a nervous break-down, I'm going to laugh. (Or break down.)

————— ◇◆◇ —————

Okay. I told you some of my glory stories. Your turn. List your best grief brain moments. Let's celebrate these as proof that your mind is doing the hard work it *should* be doing.

-

-

-

-

Creator, thank You for giving me a fully functioning mind. I need Your help with important calls, errands, and decisions. I can't do it on my own. Increase my hope that I will get my mind back someday. Until then, please cover all my slip-ups in an excessive amount of grace.

PSALM 31:9–10 • ISAIAH 26:3 • PHILIPPIANS 4:4–7 • HEBREWS 4:14–16

losing taste buds
(grief aversions)

The day after Dan's funeral was "Meet the Teacher Day" at a new school in a new town. I think shock is the only reason we were there. My children and I didn't know left from right, and somehow, in a fog, we ended up in that classroom. Of all the graces, there was another mom there who had lost her husband years prior. She told me to rest, sit down, and always keep a bottle of water and tissues nearby.

Turns out, she was right. I didn't need food. I didn't need much water. I didn't want anything sweet. Soup and shakes felt easy to digest, so that's about all I ate in small quantities, for a time.

I remember my voracious reader of a child whispering one night, "I used to love reading, Mama. But now, I've just lost the taste for it." I hear you, baby.

I met a high school girl who was in a worship band with her mom. When her mom died, she couldn't even listen to music. It was just too painful.

Maybe these precious girls will return to music and reading someday when it's less raw, and maybe not. Either way is just fine.

When there are things you kind of want to taste again, but you're nervous to do so, I call this "grief aversion."

Dancing comes to mind. It makes me feel grounded, joyful, and hopeful. But following my husband's lead was such an intimate experience that it will take great courage to step on the dance floor again. I know I will dance again. In time. And the Lord will not stop leading me, especially now that my strong and gentle leader of a husband is gone.

I couldn't even drink coffee for over two months after Dan died. Because everybody who knew Dan knew he loved French press coffee every morning. Because he even had a travel-size French press for his hardcore backpacking trips. Because part of our evening routine was the sound of the coffee grinder, preparing for the next morning, so he wouldn't wake us in the wee hours of the morning's slumber. Who knew that drinking your first cup of coffee after someone's death would be such a milestone? Death turns all kinds of things into milestones. Proof of rebuilding life, stone after stone.

I only drink coffee on special occasions. So, after Dan died, my special occasion and first cup of joe was to celebrate the fact that I was still alive and still putting one foot in front of the other, and there happened to be a coffee shop inside the grocery store. I wasn't ready yet to go to a real coffee shop without Dan, so this felt like a good baby step.

Let me tell you, buying groceries in that season was a special occasion and a huge victory. Still is. Every aisle was like a Monet of my life with Dan: the "muddy buddies," the saltines for making his favorite chicken fried steak, and the cumin for his favorite tikka masala.

The aisles held a colorful impressionistic blur of spending beautiful time with a beautiful man. Without him, life didn't have any taste left. It took me months to try to taste anything sweet and even longer to actually savor it.

But life does come back. And our taste buds do come back from the grave.

———— ◆ ————

Did you do anything out of total shock shortly after the death or funeral of your loved one that you can't believe you actually did?

What foods or activities have you lost a taste for since losing your loved one?

What big or small "firsts" have you experienced since your loved one died that felt like monumental milestones? (Like when I drank my first coffee.)

Someday, when you're ready, what do you want to do again to feel fully alive that's closely tied to the person you lost?

Can you think of a baby step to take in that direction?

God who made me, You know every part of me.
You know every craving and aversion. My whole body
aches for my loved one. Help me gain strength and eat
again. Help me find foods that feel good. While my
body needs nourishment, my soul needs hope. Please
give me a hope for my future. Give me hope for the plans
You have for me. Help me take each step one at a time.
I desperately need You.

PSALM 43:5 • PSALM 139

where can i hide?
(grief covering)

I n bed. Lights out. Eyes closed. One by one, the fears of tomor-row surround my home, march into my room, and threaten my peace. So, I do what any brave and mighty warrior would do.

I hide.

I've never hidden more in my life than since my husband died. I hide myself and my girls, our property, our loved ones. I tuck us all away in the shelter of the Most High. God's cloak covers us, and the enemy can't find us anymore.

We're hidden in Christ.

Long ago, a woman told me that fear is just smoke and mirrors. It puffs itself up to look and sound bigger than it is. We know fear is a defeated foe, but it sure can seem overpowering. When fear comes in ready to bully me and my peace, I just hide and take cover.

You know the story about Moses and the Israelites? How, through him, God told Pharaoh to set His people free, or else? That king chose ten "or else's." Swarms of bugs so thick it got dark, frogs, and plagues. But the final consequence of disobedience was death.

God also gave Moses life-saving instructions for His people: cover the top and sides of the doorframes with the blood of a lamb or a goat. The Lord would not allow the destroyer to enter their homes or harm them; it had to "pass over" those homes. (This is where the term "Passover" comes from.[1]) However, those who did not sacrifice the lamb and cover their homes with the blood lost their firstborn sons. Including Pharaoh.[2] The Bible says there has never been and never will be wailing like that in all of Egypt.[3]

Covering their doorframes with blood was an act of faith for the people. The lamb's lifeblood stood in for their own. This is also where we get the phrase "covered in the blood of Jesus." Jesus is our pure and spotless Lamb. By His blood, the consequences of eternal death pass over us. By His blood, we're set free from bondage and released to live in a promised land of freedom.

And, yet, we still live in a fallen world, and death is still a part of life. Loss can make us feel uncovered, exposed, and insecure. But Jesus covers over us. Everything we fear—it's already covered by God. He'll take care of it.

Shortly after Dan died, an old friend mailed me a necklace, a little clay rectangle stamped with a pair of wings. Underneath the wings was the word "covered." Before I went into overwhelming meetings and appointments, I wrapped a hand around the necklace, and it reminded me that I am covered by His wings. And so are my children. My loved ones. My future. My past. My finances. My concerns. My hopes. All are covered under His wings.

God's got me covered.

God chose us to be his very own through what Christ would do for us; he decided then to make us holy in his eyes, without a single fault—we who stand before him *covered with his love*. His unchanging plan has always been to adopt us into his own family by sending Jesus Christ to die for us. And he did this because he wanted to![4]

I am covered with His love . . . and so are you.

◆◆◆

We can take cover under His wings. What are your thoughts on hiding under the blood of Christ?

In what ways has your loss left you feeling uncovered, exposed, afraid, or insecure?

Can you prayerfully place the things you listed above under the blood of Jesus?

As you read the following liturgy, imagine God covering each of these things with His wings and His love.

A Liturgy of Covering
every exposed insecurity—covered
every puffed-up fear—covered
every negative imagination—covered
every moment of my past—covered
all my days ahead—covered
everyone I love and hold dear—covered
covered in the blood of Jesus.

Lamb of God, You are holy and pure. You are also my shield and fortress. I am so grateful I can hide in You when I'm afraid and feel attacked. You are my hiding place and my refuge. Help me take my thoughts, fears, and worries captive and put them under the authority of Christ. Cover all my insecurities under the blood of Jesus.

PSALM 32:7 • 1 PETER 4:8 • PSALM 91:4 • COLOSSIANS 3:1–4

i can't move
(grief fever)

New wrinkles trace and retrace my long nights and sobbing like a map on my face. I haven't showered, and I'm in pajamas. So today, my video is off for the online meeting.

The speaker became a young widow decades ago. Today she wears make-up and her hair is done; she looks rested and peaceful.

She observes, "I was only twenty-two when my husband died, but I felt a hundred years old."[1]

Wow. I am not twenty-two, but even she once felt as weary then as I do now.

This woman is hope with skin on.

One of my biggest surprises in grief is the physical penalties of it. When brokenhearted, my heart literally feels pierced and torn. Sorrow is agony across my shoulders. Loss is a trembling in my gut. Grief is also 1,000 percent exhaustion.

Grieving children often show symptoms of car sickness, tummy aches, or nightmares. I do too. Our breathing is shallow in "fight or flight" mode, and we grind our teeth at night. Sleeplessness compounds it all. Often, I cannot get out of bed. The kids arrive to school late daily. (Except that one time.) But when we can't move, we can't move.

Rosalinda explained that this is called "grief fever." That's why we need sick days and mental health days. (And if we need down days, our kids do too.)

I've experienced natural and complicated traumatic child-births, but it's possible that bearing death is more physically painful than bearing life. Grief's like the debilitating state of severe postpartum depression . . . but it lasts much longer. People expect me to bounce back after a month or two. They expect me to be able to spell my name correctly and answer simple questions and even be able to drive. And I just can't.

I've learned to value stretch marks from childbearing by calling them glory marks. Will I ever see grief wrinkles as glory lines? I don't know.

At the end of a long day, I look at my half-sentence journal entry from this morning. My first response is to laugh.[2]

I woke up

This was as far as I got in my quiet morning moment. I laugh because I didn't even get to finish this sentence. The second half is missing. There's no punctuation, which actually seems fitting right now. We are in a semicolon season between what was and what is to come; our story isn't finished yet.

But as I reassess my lot, my day, the boundary lines drawn around me, and the responsibilities on my plate, I no longer snicker at myself. As my day winds down and sweet potatoes roast in the oven, I reconsider my self-laughter. I see how Grace Himself sees me.

I think about how deeply profound this statement actually is:

I woke up

And I think about how deeply profound it is that my feet kept taking steps and my mind kept making calls and my children made it to the doctor's and we snuggled up to watch *Cat in the Hat* and jammed to "Burn the Ships" and prayed and battled. It can only be proof of God's grace when we can't complete a basic sentence and then we run a full run-on-sentence kind of day. How in the world did I accomplish all that today?

I woke up

Grace carries me. There's no other possible explanation.

I woke up

And that alone proves that Resurrection power lives in me.

And you woke up too. Reading this is proof. Resurrection power lives in you too.

> "Wake up, sleeper,
> Rise from the dead
> And Christ will shine on you."[3]

Many days, I wake up and just lie flat in bed all day. Those days are grace too. Because when we can't move, God is working a profound healing in our bodies and souls. It's a mending work that takes a careful, slow, and steady stitch. He's putting the left brain back together with the right brain, renewing our mind after trauma and loss split us in two.

There's grace for the physical pain and grace for days we can't budge. God can move mountains that won't budge and raise up dry bones from the ash heap. And He's so kind to just hold us there some days too, requiring nothing of us, offering the ministry of His quiet presence.

A big part of the rebuilding we'll do together in this book happens here in the question-and-answer section. The whole narrative leads up to this moment. It's where you'll process everything you just read and begin to put the pieces of your heart and life back together. Take your time, reflect on them throughout your week, and record answers as they come to you:

What's one of your biggest surprises in grief?

How would you explain what grief feels like to you? Where and how does grief or trauma manifest in your body?

Do you know anyone who has lost and survived and are now your "hope with skin on"?

God of Resurrection, thank You for the gift of waking up.
Thank You for grace to rebuild and rest. Thank You for
another day. Please help me take deep breaths and long
exhales. Fill me with Your Spirit, and give me my
breath back. Please bring healing to these places in
my bones and sinews that carry such anguish. In the
face of death, bring me back to life.

MATTHEW 11:28–30 • PHILIPPIANS 3:10–11 • JOHN 20:22 • EZEKIEL 37:6–9

moving forward
(grief courage)

On our first bike ride without Daddy after moving to Colorado, I flashed back to our previous duty stations together. Bike rides down the beach to get frozen custard and past cornfields to get pizza. *Together.* The memories were bittersweet. The mountains in the background . . . they too were bittersweet. (Every good thing is right now.) People often tell me, "You'll never move on. But you do move forward." I guess it's because we have to move forward and rebuild, whether we want to or not.

I call this "grief courage."

Going to church was another brave pedal forward. I longed for our old church family, feeling known and loved; but in a new town, everyone was new. Military wives know how to jump in and make friends, and I knew we needed community more than ever. But it took every ounce of emotional, physical, and spiritual strength to get my body into church, in hopes of building community from the ground up. (Again.)

On Wednesday night, the pastor told us to raise our hands if we needed prayer, so we'd know we weren't alone. "Look around, lay hands on, and pray for the people who need it." In a new church, the memory of our old church's motto comforted me, "No one fights alone." I'd never felt more alone in my life, so I raised my hand high. But no one put their hand on my shoulder. I even turned around and told the guy behind me, desperately, "I need a hand." He heard me, made eye contact, but he didn't budge.

Abandoned, alone, and surrounded by a thousand people.

After that time of prayer for each other, we entered into worship. My daughter wanted to move forward to the altar where we used to worship with Daddy. I could tell this was important for her heart, so I bravely squeezed through crowded aisles, making our way to the front. That was hard for my meek personality, but if I'm honest, I wanted to be there too. I felt like Dan was waiting at the altar for us like he did at our old church. When we finally made it to the front, I just collapsed to my knees. I wept and wept and wept.

I missed the fire and fellowship of our old church. But I came forward that day to worship the Lord, and I did so with my tears. By the end, several people introduced themselves and a few prayed over me and offered to help us.

We were suddenly surrounded but no longer alone.

Even though it countered my comfort level, moving forward was the difference between begging for help alone and being surrounded with hope of finding a new community. You may experience times where your community, authorities, or church will look you in the eye, hear your pleas for help, and then look the other way. My heart (and God's heart) breaks for you when that happens.

But our options are simple. We can withdraw, self-isolate, and become bitter. Or we can forgive and move forward. Sometimes, moving forward means moving on to find others who are willing to step in and help.

Moving forward in the literal sense (thanks to my daughter's courageous and sincere request) was also a spiritual moving forward. In that moment, I left the bullies of rejection and abandonment behind. And I stepped forward into praise and worship.

Something amazing happens when we stop trying to find our source of comfort in people and start seeking God's presence instead. Somehow, in God's economy, when we seek Him first, He provides everything else we need.[1] Lord knows I need community. But ironically, seeking God alone opened the door to that hopeful glimmer of community.

◆

Let's celebrate some of your pedals forward together.

What have you done to rebuild and live life again that felt really brave? (Honestly, getting out of bed feels brave most days; don't discount those things too.)

People can easily bruise us in our loss. Have you also felt abandoned, avoided, or rejected in your grief? Tell me about it:

How can you bravely move toward healing?

Consider finding a local grief support group, GriefShare, TAPS, or DivorceCare. Give it a chance. You may find it surprisingly helpful, no matter how recently or long ago you lost your loved one.

> Courageous One, everything I do right now feels brave.
> Getting up in the morning. Going to the grocery store.
> Going on a walk. Going to church. Give me courage.

MATTHEW 6:33 • DEUTERONOMY 31:8

who am i anymore?
(grief + identity)

Loss changes everything about who we are, doesn't it? Our needs, hopes, wants, desires, faith, identity, and even personality. Consequences I didn't see coming.

Loving Dan changed me deeply and profoundly. He taught me healthy communication. He taught me how to be loved, adored, and forgiven. A once very strong-willed, stubborn woman transformed into a surrendered, secure, happy-to-follow partner. His love changed me.

Only a few months in, I was already noticing the ways losing Dan was changing me too. I was learning to fight for justice and be more decisive. I find I'm even more like Dan now that he is gone.

And then there's the ever-present identity piece—from military to civilian, married to single, co-parent to solo mom, dependent to primary. Each of these slaps me in the face as I find myself in new social situations. I will not minimize the jarring difficulty of how loss changes our identities in one tragic moment. And yet, we can't ever fully entrust our identities to things that are temporary. Grief included.

Widow is a temporary identity. But child of God is forever.

> **Widow is a temporary identity. But child of God is forever.**

48

Grief has a way of shaking our temporary identities to the core, leaving kingdom identities standing firm. At the end of the day, "all of creation will be shaken and removed, so that only unshakable things will remain."[1] That's why leaning into your identity as a child of God is so grounding and anchoring. His love for you will never be shaken nor removed even when everything else falls to pieces.[2] Our identity is forgiven, loved, accepted, and cherished. While that truth softens the blow, it does not hide us entirely from the sting.

I bet the most bitter, victimized people you know have experienced deep loss. Interestingly, the most beautiful, humble souls you know are probably people who experienced great loss too. Sorrow can either define us as victims or it can refine us into the image of God. We have a choice.

I feel pretty humbled and honored to be following behind those who've experienced deep grief, folks who are well-acquainted with sorrow. They've become gentle and lowly in spirit like Jesus. If we have to walk through the Valley of the Shadow, at least let us turn out like them.

Loving and losing Dan has and will always change me deeply. In ways yet to be discovered, I'm certain. And still, loving Christ has and will forever change me the deepest. Christ has set His fiery, loving gaze upon me, and I cannot help but return His affection.

Take some time this week to reflect on how loving and losing has changed who you are—for better or for worse. It's okay if it's not all peaches and cream. We still have plenty of time to heal and transition from our losses defining us to refining us.

Write your loved one's name in the blanks below then complete the sentence. Add more discoveries over time.

Ways loving _____ changed me:

Ways losing _____ changed me:

What do you think is the difference between the bereaved who become bitter and those who become a blessing to others?

When have you felt like a victim? Are you letting victimization take root in places where you've been legitimately hurt?

God of creation, I hardly recognize myself these days,
but You understand me intimately. Help me sort out
the changes, within and around me. I'm not who I was,
and I never will be again. Beautiful places in me died
when my beloved died. Resurrect dead seeds.
Prune off the toxic things rearing their heads.
Replace the dead branches with new life in Christ.
You promise that in Christ, I'm a new creation.
If I have to become someone else through this loss,
let it be a humbler, more compassionate,
and more gracious version of me.
Let it make me more like Jesus.

HEBREWS 12:26–29 • JOHN 1:12–13 • JOB 23:10–11 • MATTHEW 11:29

PART TWO

THE TOPOGRAPHY OF GRIEF

(what to expect)

mapping sorrow

People read a map in at least two different ways. Some want to know, "How do I get from point A to B? What is the quickest route? And where are my pit stops along the way?" Their purpose is planning. (That was my husband.) Others look at a map with awe and say, "Wow. Isn't that beautiful?" They hang the map on their wall for decoration or cut hearts out of it to make scrapbooks. Their purpose is admiration. For them, a map is something to behold—the rich colors, textures, and elevations. They're also not as concerned with the finish line as they're concerned about the character they build along the way. (That's me.)

Both perspectives have great value. But with grief, trying to plan and time and zip through the path will only frustrate you more.

On our grief journey, when we focus on, "Who will I become?" instead of "How fast can I get out of here?" then we gain a whole new appreciation for the Valley of the Shadow.

For his birthday one year, I got Dan a map of Colorado's fifty-three peaks since he wanted to hike them all. It was different from the detailed maps he used to plan hiking routes with his copious notes of the trail. Instead of a planning map, this one invited us to admire the bigger picture of creation: memories of stunning peaks he already explored with God and dreams of future peaks to summit.

If we can frame grief more like the map of Colorado's fourteeners, we can appreciate the beauty, the various paths, and the highs and lows. Since grief is not linear and cannot be planned or timed, an A-to-B map will do us no good. We can't chart the start to the finish as quickly as possible. But we can get a rough idea of what we might encounter on the journey. We can understand the lay

my map of sorrow

of the land: *How does grief work? What can I expect? How do I get through this?*

Grief is a normal part of life, just like marriage, parenting, and career planning. We don't get step-by-step road maps for any of the most important parts of life. But we do have access to familiar pathways and disciplines that will help us navigate one step at a time through the new terrain. Understanding the lay of the land will reduce frustration, increase peace, and make our strenuous trek less daunting.

———— ⋄◆⋄ ————

Let's figure out where you are on the map. What are your biggest frustrations with grief?

How do you relate most to maps? For planning or admiration?

If you could stop wanting an A-to-B route and start appreciating grief for its elevations, what do you think would change for you?

Take another look at my Map of Sorrow doodle. What realms, milestones, or hurdles would you include in your own Map of Sorrow?

In the box, draw your Map of Sorrow. Picture some everyday symbols of your grief right now. This will change over time.

For example, you could sketch a tree for Paperwork Forest, a bake pan for Casserole Cavern, or a teardrop for Counseling Mountain. For inspiration, search online for maps of *The Chronicles of Narnia* or *The Hobbit*. Need a simpler example? Think *Dora the Explorer*. "Say it with me!"[1] Insomnia, Puffy Eyes, Journaling! (In other words, draw two obstacles and a milestone to reach.)

Don't worry about your artistry because we celebrate stick-figures around here. This is for your brain, heart, and soul (not a grade).

my grief map:

Please share your map with me and encourage your fellow companions in sorrow. Tag me @companioninsorrow and be sure to use #whenmountainscrumble. If you're struggling to get started on your map, that's a great place to find inspiration too!

Lord, You are the trailblazer. You go before us. You create new pathways where there is currently no way.[2] While there may not be a formula I can follow, I can always follow You. Take my hand and lead me. The Valley of the Shadow of Death is not a place I ever wanted to be. But it seems I have no choice. At least I do not have to go it alone. Hold me. Sit with me. Carry me. Weep with me. Help me breathe. Show me how to find my footing. I need You, Holy Spirit. Come.

ISAIAH 43:15–19 • PSALM 23:1–4

the wave pool

Celebrating life after a loved one's death feels both courageous and conflicting. After Dan died, we played at a waterpark to celebrate one of our first family birthdays without him. Our waterpark tickets were a gift from a generous woman who understood what it was like to lose her dad at a young age, and she had not even met our family yet! I liked the waterslides best, but my girls wanted to ride the waves in the crowded wave pool. The entire jostling time felt like a download from God, a modern-day parable to help me understand what we're going through.

First, *proximity matters.*

The waves from the front of the pool near the wave machine are much bigger and more intense. Similarly, in grief, the closer you are to the person who died, the harder the waves will hit you. Even if you're on the far end of the pool and only knew them from a distance, you will still feel the waves. Just more mildly.

Stance matters.

In the wave pool, if you try to just stand up like normal, the waves will slam harder against you and likely knock you over. It hurts if you try to fight it. As you grieve, you have to surrender to the waves and ride them, or they'll knock you down.

Anticipation matters.

When you see a wave coming, you crouch low and get ready on the lull. Then you jump up in order to move with the wave when it threatens to pull you under. When you anticipate the waves caused by upcoming milestones and triggers, then you can focus on your surroundings, listen to your body, and try to move with the waves. That makes it a little easier when the waves hit.

But sometimes, a wave will slam against you that you cannot foresee. Without warning, it knocks you over anyway. If you don't get up again, you'll drown. So, you get back up again.

Endurance matters.

The longer the waves keep coming and coming, the harder it is to keep going and going. You begin to feel woozy and exhausted. You have less and less ability to gauge how long each round of waves might last. Even when you're looking straight at the clock over the lifeguard's head, time becomes a blur. With time, either you grow stronger to manage the waves better or the waves become smaller and have less power. I don't know which. Either way, hang in there. You're going to make it.

People around you matter.

The behavior of the adults, teens, and children around you in a wave pool can either compound or alleviate your stress. If they're attentive and aware of their surroundings, their presence can be a real comfort. They may even look out for your kids if they see one dipping under. However, if the people around you prove reckless and throw themselves around, without regard to how their coping behavior affects others, their presence is a real threat.

Watchfulness matters.

If you have children or you're a caregiver, the waves require extra vigilance and endurance. You're on higher alert for your own waves but also for theirs, making sure your children's heads don't go under the water if they incorrectly time the ups and downs. This is necessary and exhausting. Raising grieving children, while you're also grieving, requires incredible focus and fortitude. You can't think about anything else but the next wave. (That explains grief brain.) Survival is number one. Frills and extracurriculars no longer matter because this is a long game.

Laughter matters.

You'll be surprised how much your children still giggle and have fun. You'll laugh and smile too. Some days you're on high alert, ensuring you make it out alive. But other days, even in the stress and chaos and navigating the unruly people around you, you'll find laughter remains. There can still be joy.

Respite matters.

Be thankful for those moments when you get to take a break from the waves. Don't fill that time with busyness or fruitless hurry. There are gaps for a reason, and this is grace. Rest in the lulls. More waves are likely coming.

Lifeguards matter.

Ask counselors, mentors, family, and friends to watch out for you and your kids. Let them know you might go under at any moment. Let others help shoulder the hypervigilance. This provides a real covering of safety and a breath of relief. You will rest easier knowing you have watchmen on the walls, both in prayer and in physical support.

Lifeguards matter. Again.

When I found myself exhausted and wondering if I could keep this up, I started paying attention to the eyes of the lifeguard. I knew I couldn't keep all my people safe, so I put my confidence in the lifeguard. His eyes scanned the waves from left to right, checking to see if anyone needed to be rescued. In grief, being on alert for myself and my family is exhausting. But we can rest knowing that there is always a Savior with a better vantage point, whose eyes roam the earth, to and fro, watching out for those He loves.

Grace matters.

Even if you're positioned and alert, set your lifeguards in place, and rest between waves, you can still get an unexpected slap in the face. In those moments, our best option is to lean on grace to get us through. Even when it's all too much, Grace Himself is still enough.

———— ◆ ————

Let's come up for some air.

When you think of surviving the waves of sorrow, can you think of other things that matter?

From the list of what matters, which matters to you most in your waves of grief right now?

Describe how the waves are hitting you today. Date today's entry because this will change over time.

God of the waves, mighty things happen when You say, "Peace, be still." While I cannot make the waves of my grief stop, I ask You to put peace, endurance, and resolve within me to calm the storm inside. Please set watchmen and lifeguards in place, through prayer and practical means. Alert Your people to pray for me when I'm going under and to keep watch over me and my family. Even when I sleep, You're attentive and praying over me. Help me rest in that.

LUKE 8:22–25 • 2 CHRONICLES 16:9 • GALATIANS 6:2 • PSALM 121:3–4

the faulty five stages

If ever a truth set you free in loss, let it be this one: there are no stages of grief. There is no formula, no five-step process, and therefore no "right way" to grieve.

I had a visceral reaction when I first heard of the "five stages of grief": from denial and isolation, to anger, to bargaining, to depression, to acceptance.[1] Everything in me wanted to scream. *Stupid stages!* I've observed my own grieving long enough to know it doesn't happen like that.

In the first week of loss, I experienced high doses of both denial and acceptance. If the stages exist, then how could I go from acceptance to anger within fifteen minutes and then be all over the place for fifteen months? I felt anger but never bargained. I experienced devastation but not depression. The five-stage model left me wondering, "I don't feel depressed. Is something wrong with me?" Can we just laugh at the irony?

These stages can make us second-guess ourselves, wondering if we're grieving the wrong way. But if you're within the boundaries of love, there is no wrong way to grieve.

Elisabeth Kübler-Ross was the psychiatrist who first introduced the idea of five stages in her book *On Death and Dying: What the Dying Have to Teach Doctors, Nurses, Clergy & Their Own Families*. However, she wasn't referring to people grieving the loss of a loved one at all![2] Her research noted the stages a *patient* goes through when they face *their own* mortality. Kübler-Ross's study was a "discussion of some key emotional reactions to the experience of the dying. . . . grief was a part of that experience, but it was not the totality of the experience."[3] Unfortunately, even fifty years after she wrote this book, these five stages are still being misapplied to almost any and every form of grief.

Turns out I'm not the only grieving person who doesn't follow the stage model (at all). Researchers on an international scale confirm the lack of evidence for specific grief stages. "A mistaken belief in the stage model . . . can have devastating consequences. Not only can it lead bereaved persons to feel that they are not coping appropriately," it can also prevent them from getting the care and support they need.[4] Researchers explain that believing in grief stages places a false expectation on grieving people to move from one reaction to the next in "a more orderly fashion than usually occurs." Worse, it can lead to "hasty assessments of where individuals are or ought to be in the grieving process."[5] This might even be a reason why friends, family, and doctors respond in "unhelpful and potentially harmful" ways.[6]

Toward the end of her career, Kübler-Ross and her partner regretted that their work was so commonly misrepresented and misapplied[7]:

> The stages have evolved since their introduction, and they have been very misunderstood over the past three decades. They were never meant to help tuck messy emotions into neat packages. They are responses to loss that many people have, but there is not a typical response to loss, as there is no typical loss. Our grief is as individual as our lives.[8]

Grief isn't as linear, tidy, or formulaic as we've been misled to expect. Grief can't be compartmentalized, categorized, or sanitized.

Grief can get messy. Therefore, people who are uncomfortable with emotions latch on to the five stages of grief because a formula feels safer and more predictable. We're so "scientific" and want to know what to expect. Grief will knock your scientific socks off.

Because these stages have been so widely adopted in our culture, it's easy to think:

I don't feel depressed. Am I doing this wrong?

I feel angry today. Oh no. I must be entering the (dreaded) "angry stage."

And it's even worse when other people try to fit us into these stages.

Oh, my son. He's in the "bargaining stage."

Listen to her. She must still be in the denial stage.

It's unfair to ask the bereaved to give a progress report.

Listen. The only predictable thing about grief is its unpredictability.

For me, grief can look like laughing because I remember Dan's goofy dance and, five seconds later, I'm sobbing on the floor unable to breathe, and then I'm punching the pillow because I'm so mad. This range of emotion can happen within three minutes or three hours or three days. And then I'm fine (for a couple hours or a couple days or a couple weeks) until I'm laid flat on the couch because I just can't even . . . just can't even . . . can't even finish a sentence, read a paragraph, or see straight. And I can't even believe this is happening. *Or why?!*

But I get it. It can feel scary to not have a formula because then we fear there might not be a solution. While we may not have stages to follow and boxes to check, we do have a Shepherd to follow and a hand to hold. Following after Jesus is intimate and healing in a way that following a five-step progression can never be.

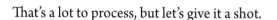

That's a lot to process, but let's give it a shot.

What have you been told about the "five stages of grief"?

Does hearing that there are no formulaic stages relieve you or disappoint you? Why do you think that is?

Have you ever second-guessed yourself and your process of grief? If so, what triggers that second-guessing? Has anything ever made you wonder, "Am I the only one that's reacting like this?"

Have you made a decision to follow after Jesus toward healing or have you been trying to follow a manmade path out of grief?

Comforter, lift off this extra pressure and expectation surrounding how I'm grieving. Relieve me from wondering, "Is feeling this way normal? Am I doing it the right way?" Give me freedom to say instead, "This is where I'm at, and it's right where I need to be. This is what I feel, and it's exactly what I need to feel." I entrust my emotions, fears, questions, and next steps to You. Increase my trust in You. I don't love feeling like there's no pathway or formula to follow. All I can do is take Your hand as You lead me through this valley. I give You my heart. Be the leader of my life. I want to follow You.

PSALM 95:6–7 • PSALM 25:5–6, 9 • ISAIAH 40:11

sippy cups and avoidance

Jesus says, "Blessed are those who mourn, for they will be comforted."[1]

Yes. But what if we choose not to mourn? Then how can anyone comfort us?

Mourning is different from grief: it's the public and communal expression of internal sorrow. Mourning is crying with a friend or wearing a memorial band around your arm or a pin on your lapel. Mourning is the bumper sticker that says we'll never forget you or the combat boots by the front door. It's the Facebook post that shares what your person meant to you or how you're celebrating or struggling with various milestones. These are public displays of our internal pain that communicate to others that we are hurting.

Mourning is a vulnerable and indirect invitation that says, "I'm grieving, and I don't want to grieve alone." So, if we don't mourn, if we don't risk the hurt, how can anyone even try to comfort us? Even within our own hearts, we keep busy, thus forfeiting comfort from God because we are scared the pain might pull us under.

Everyone says you can't go around grief. You have to go through it. But we try, don't we? And when we try, we often find more of an offense than a comfort.

Avoiding grief is that stink in your car that you can't pinpoint until weeks later. You search, but it takes a while to locate the culprit. You suspect a dead rodent until you find the sippy cup of milk that has rolled under the driver's seat and soured in the heat of summer. Once you've discovered and exposed it, you can finally deal with it, clean out your car, and drive around to let in some fresh air.

What we avoid will wait patiently for us. Your body will tell you that you're not okay even if you ignore your emotions or mind. If you rush, stuff, or ignore grief, you will have to deal with it eventually. Buried deep and harder to identify, the longer it waits, it just might come out stinking worse later on. If you've already experienced this, it's okay. You're not the first person to try to avoid your grief; you won't be the last. And there's always grace for it.

I am naturally a confronter, wanting to resolve my junk as quickly as possible. But trauma and grief don't always work on our timelines, and sometimes they don't even behave according to our personality traits. My screaming, swearing, and wailing have shocked me at times. And definitely those around me.

Sometimes trauma keeps the grief buried so we can deal with it later when we have more emotional safety nets in place. With all of our moves and school changes and administrative chaos, even the PTSD didn't hit us until the one-year anniversary of his death. The heart and mind wait patiently for healing while you're in the thick of both fight and flight. Don't feel ashamed when your grief work needs to be avoided or postponed. But know that eventually, you will have to let sorrow work its way through you. One way or another, one day or another.

I encourage myself by remembering the attractive, magnetic humility and gentle-heartedness I've witnessed in people acquainted with sorrow. It reminds me that there's deep healing available to me if I don't lose heart and don't avoid the grief work. Those who walked the valley before me have been changed— changed in a kingdom way. They see with eyes eternal and they give with hearts open wide. And while I wish bereavement wasn't my path, I constantly feel humbled and honored to be trailing behind such beautiful people.

Healing from grief isn't about finding a way to numb the pain, avoid the loss, or jump through hoops to get out of it. If we avoid the grief work and the mourning, we not only forfeit the comfort but also the healing. Healing from grief is more of a becoming—becoming a new, refined version of you without the one you loved by your side anymore.

Do you naturally confront or avoid your grief work?

Have you let out a wail yet? Did that surprise you? Did it help release some things? Perhaps you never wail, and that's okay too.

Has anything compounded your loss and put you in fight or flight mode? Record them here so you can remember to give yourself grace when your grief work feels stalled, tabled, or postponed.

If you've been avoiding grief on purpose, can you articulate why?

Does the hope of who you might become compel you to begin the grief work and find the healing?

God of comfort, come quickly to my side.
I need the comfort of Your nearness. Give me a grace
and a courage to embrace sobbing, anger, laughter.
And then, God, give me grace to bring it to You.
You are still the God who brings beauty from ashes,
joy from despair. If I have to go through this valley,
let it gently change and shape who I am. Let me become
like Jesus, with an attractive humility and a
magnetic gentleness of heart.

MATTHEW 5:4 • PSALM 34:18 • ISAIAH 61:1–3 • JOB 23:8–11

feast or famine

God delights in feeding His children sweet bread when we're lost in the wilderness. I must be learning what it means to live off of daily bread too.

Today, my daily bread was named Megan. A total stranger who stopped at my table at a coffee shop and said, "Are you okay?" God's familiar kindness was in her eyes. The same kindness Dan carried in his eyes. So I was honest.

"No. I am not okay." She prayed for me right then and there. The first time someone has looked me in the eyes, laid hands on me, and prayed out loud over me in a very, very long time. The thing I miss and long for most. Being carried to heaven when I'm too weary to get there on my own.

The first sentence she spoke to the Lord was especially anointed, "Father, take this mountain from her." Downpours of tears flooded the table, the mountain of bills, the desert of to-do lists.

After today, I'm asking for daily bread.

He's not feeding me more than I need; I'm honestly feeling quite rationed. But I have what I need for the day. Tomorrow, He'll have to show up and feed me again. I've got no word or fore-taste of tomorrow's bread. (Because it's still today.) And this is all I get for now.

And if His Word holds true, then this is also all I need for now. I lack no good thing, He says.[1] Oh, you bet I'm begging for chicken fried steak, mashed potatoes, cream gravy, and fried okra. I want that buffet of richest of fare. I want the milk and honey. But for now . . . *The Bread of Affliction.*

And then I hear that familiar, faint whisper. One I have not heard in a very, very long time. One I long for and miss. He promises to lead me to safety, "to rescue me because he delights in me."[2] Maybe that's the last bit of nourishment I need to top off my hungry belly in order to fall asleep?

Grief is feast or famine. Either you're up to your elbows in casseroles (if you're lucky) or pizza or rotisserie chicken . . . or your cupboards are bare and you can't find strength to order groceries and why bother because you're not that hungry anyway. You're saturated in texts and phone calls, but then, when you really need somebody, it's you and crickets.

For months when I brushed my teeth at night, I tried to think really hard, "Did I talk to another adult today?" My days were excruciatingly lonely and solitary. If you know what that's like, I'm so sorry. Every now and then, people popped in and out. But Dan . . .

Dan was my steady and constant. Even deployed or traveling, I knew I could email him or talk with him and depend on him. Without him, there's desert and mudslides. There's no morning mist. Only drought and then torrential rain.

Manna feels rationed and then we feel overwhelmed at the bounty. I don't have any great wisdom on what to do about it. But just recognizing that this is the nature of loss *for almost everybody I know* helps me feel less "poor, poor pitiful me." It helps me understand that I'm just at the mercy of feast and famine.

In feast, I try to freeze some of it and save it for later. I write down the blessings or the provisions so I can live off of them for as long as possible. In famine, I encourage my soul by remembering those times that God and people *did* come through for me. I encourage you to do the same.

Where are you at today? Feast or famine?

Can you remember the last gush of provision? Write the comforts down so you can remember them later.

Bread of Life, nourish me in the middle of this affliction.
Minister to me in ways only You can. Send me just the
right people at just the right time. Send me help and
provision when I need it. Thank You for sustaining me
with just what I need each day. In Jesus' name, amen.

PSALM 34:10 • JOHN 6:57–58 • PSALM 78:25

switchbacks and setbacks

They say time heals all wounds. But it doesn't. Time cannot do that. Only the heavenly Father can heal all wounds.

Nonetheless, we'd like to know if we are progressing or regressing on our grief timeline, right? But I don't think it works that way. Sometimes in sorrow, going back is going forward.

A friend, Shelley, explained that thirty years after losing her grandma, she's still circling back and receiving new levels of healing through counseling. She likened the pain of grief to the sore feeling you get when you ride your bike or lift weights or kick box. It's a good sore. But it still hurts. That's exactly it.

Three months after I lost my husband, a woman said to me, "Well, I'm sure it just gets a little bit easier every day." I wanted to yell, "Are you kidding me? It gets *harder* every single day!" It takes time to reveal all we've lost. My friend John explained it this way: "Losing a spouse is devastating in ways that my eyes have just recently been partially opened to. I say 'partially' as each day brings new reminders of what Bethany meant to me and how much deeper the wound is than I realized."[1]

> Time can't heal all wounds, but it can slowly reveal wounds that we need to carry to the Father for healing.

His words minister to me because it's true. Each day and new circumstance reveal how Dan's absence is even deeper than we previously felt or understood. Daily, we learn more of how much Dan meant to us and just how much he did to love, bless, provide for, protect, and bring joy to our family. Time can't heal all wounds, but it can slowly reveal wounds that we need to carry to the Father for healing, little by little.[2]

When hiking fourteeners, a switchback is a trail that zig-zags back and forth up the mountain. This takes more time, but it allows your body to acclimate and endure. Switchbacks make a hike safer and more manageable. If a hiker tries to go straight up the mountain, it will prove dangerous or impossible. The body just can't do that.

This is grace to the grieving: we don't feel all the loss all at once.

We have to go little by little, back and forth. We want to go back to revisit that place or open up those old love letters, but we just can't yet. We want to move forward and try dancing again, but we just can't yet. The mind and body know how to pace themselves. They force you to stop sometimes. This is not a problem; it's a protection. We can only handle so much jarring reality at a time.

Moving forward seems to require some degree of looking backward. This helps us come to peace with our memories. But there are some memory lanes I'm not ready to hike again. Others are life-giving highways that I'd like the courage to get back on again. That's why I can't go back to those mountains. Not yet anyway. Maybe not ever. That's okay. It's another type of aversion. It's a red flag in your body or your soul that says, "Nope. I can't go down that path. Not yet. Not today."

Today, we're just marking the trail. We don't have to do the deep healing now, but we want to note the aversions on our maps because they're clues to places that we'll need to revisit someday. These red flags and grief aversions are junctures in our souls where we'll want to invite the Lord to restore, redeem, and rebuild. (Someday, when we're ready.)

It's good to switch back and forth between our joy and our sorrow. This makes the trek more manageable. So balance marking the trail with looking at how far you've come. And fix your eyes on the joy and the heavenlies in front of you. There's still dreams to dream and hopes to hope. There's still life to live. And yes, there's still time to spend. While time might not heal me, I know well the God who can.

———— ♦♦♦ ————

Are there songs, scriptures, activities, or routines you can't handle without your loved one right now? Are there boxes or drawers you'd like to unpack, emails or letters to read ... someday, but not yet?

Are there any locations you can't yet return to? Why don't you want to go back there?

On the other hand, which places or phrases, routines, activities, songs, or scriptures do you keep returning to, like retracing your steps, so you can relive the good memories?

Close your eyes and remember a time you felt comforted, safe, and secure. Write down details about that moment and relive it as often as you need to. Even memories minister to us.

Father, help me be honest with myself and with You.
As things come to my memory throughout the days
ahead, help me take note. Help me identify what feels
triggering. Help me mark the path so that someday,
when I'm ready, You can breathe life and redemption
back over these ashes. And show me steps I can
retrace that will bring comfort and peace to me.

PSALM 147:3 • PSALM 27:13–14 • 2 PETER 3:9

PART THREE

FIND YOUR FOOTING

(soul-care)

life-giving list

It's often explained that the most highly stressful life events are the death of a loved one, divorce, and moving. During the height of the pandemic, after losing my husband and moving to three locations within three months (and when cars and appliances and everything else kept breaking), I decided to take a stress inventory test.[1] It's an understatement to say my numbers were literally off the charts. Somehow, this felt affirming. Apparently, I *am* under a high amount of stress, and that helps me give myself grace when I'm not always able to keep my cool.

The problem is that my results didn't give me any wisdom or action steps. It only told me that my body was highly susceptible to illness after enduring such distress. *Thanks a lot.* It felt like the results just gave me a "false prophecy" of sorts about my health. That test doesn't have authority to declare anything about my future or my health.

So, I took a red pen and (heatedly) scribbled over the whole test. I wrote over everything on that list of stressors in huge letters: "The Blood of Jesus." Like how the Israelites painted the blood of the lamb on their doorposts at Passover and it protected them from the spirit of death. I used red ink to symbolically cover all those stressors and the test results in His blood and prayed He would wash them white as snow.

They say that you're more likely to get in car wrecks in the first couple years after loss. Driving is a difficult task when your mind isn't working at full capacity and your body is exhausted. (I do often wonder if the light I just drove through was even green.) They say that you may have all kinds of health problems later. They say you will lose or gain weight or that you'll get depressed. But should we believe these "sayings"?

It does us no good to put our faith in these imagined negative futures, so I take these thoughts captive immediately by bringing them to God in prayer.[2] Instead of just believing what "they say," we can use this info to our benefit. Acknowledging the reality of our stressful situations can motivate us to act in ways to care for ourselves (like hitching a ride instead of driving ourselves, increasing our driving insurance coverage, or setting reminders on our phone to actually eat dinner.)

Stress levels may be through the roof, but when put under the feet of Jesus, they won't debilitate us (forever). When I feel the cortisol pumping and I start acting like a cranky mama or a frazzled friend, it's usually because I've forgotten what's life-giving and have let those things slide. It's easy to forget about doing the foundational things that bring us life when all we can think of is the death of our loved one. In those seasons, I've found a simple practice that reorients my soul and brings me great peace: I write my Life-Giving List.

Here are a few examples of what you might put on your list:

- stretching

- journaling

- laughing

- calling a friend

- getting to bed early

- laying on the couch

- bike riding

- getting a massage

- soaking in a Scripture

- praying in the shower

- doodling

After you write your life-giving list, put it somewhere obvious, maybe on your kitchen cupboard or near your calendar. When super stressed, review your list and reassess if you're actually *doing* these life-giving things to reduce stress levels.

Making life-giving choices doesn't mean you're self-absorbed. So don't let guilt or condemnation try to talk you out of this. It brings me a lot of life to write for others. It brings me a lot of life to cook for others. It brings me life to intercede for others.

My list changes depending on the season because my life now is entirely different than the life I lived three years ago. Which is why I desperately need to rewrite my Life-Giving List all over again, from scratch. Like everything else in my life. Scratch.

Thankfully, our God is the God who makes something out of nothing and beautiful things from scratch. Thankfully, even while navigating our loved one's death, we are still able to fill our lists with activities that bring us life.

Now the fun part. It's your turn. Write your Life-Giving List and put it somewhere for easy reference when you feel stressed. It will help you refocus your time and energy.

my life-giving list:

-

-

-

-

-

-

-

-

-

What activities, routines, or thought patterns do you currently practice that bring you life, peace, or joy?

What brings you life that serves others?

If you want to print out the stress test, it may prove affirming to see where you're at. However, don't forget to take your red marker and cover the test, both figuratively and prayerfully, in the blood of Jesus.

You get the final say, Lord. Breathe life into me. Show me ways I can de-stress and maintain the upswing. Lead me to activities that usher in peace, joy, and hope.

ISAIAH 46:4 • PROVERBS 18:21

lilies and resilience

Every stem, leaf, and lily collapsed over the edge of the large white pot from the weight and the neglect. Such beauty, strength, and splendor doubled over in a heap. Whenever I noticed the lilies in such poor shape, I watered them. Astoundingly, they always perked back up overnight. Tall, strong, and chin lifted high.

One day, Samwise came to help me replace my busted alternator. He's one of my companions in the thick of sorrow like me. His quiet presence reminds me I'm not alone. We sat at the kitchen table with a cup of tea and discussed how many times my peace lilies have collapsed and recovered since my aunt gave them to me after my husband died. The plant seems to die and come back to life again, over and over, a constant reminder of the Resurrection.

"It's a good grief plant," Samwise remarked.

I can't shake that phrase: *good grief plant.* I think he meant it's good for a grieving household because it's so forgiving and resilient. I clearly can't tend to her needs attentively right now. But I think there's more to it. I imagine the leaves like arms lifted high in worship and the lilies praising their Maker. Then she withers and stoops low in lament.

Suddenly, I see myself in her. I double over weeping, collapsing on the couch. With a little water, rest, and sunshine, I'm upright the next day.

Up and down. Up and down.

Today, the plant is wilting again. It's been a while, several months actually, since I let the plant completely double over. This tells me that I'm doing better too.

The ups and downs aren't as extreme as in the beginning. I've learned to recognize when the plant needs water sooner, before she completely crumples. When I notice the signs now, I actually have the strength and wits about me to water and care for her.

A little water powerfully strengthens that plant overnight! But in my life, what does watering practically look like?

Sabbath rest.

I'm visibly and physically wilting by the end of another demanding week. But after a full day off from social media, screens, work, and chores, I wake the next day totally refreshed.

Eating. Anything.

Grieving is the season for comfort foods. When your body is in fight or flight, your stomach can't digest like normal. I'm no doctor, but don't beat yourself up for wanting mashed potatoes. The body needs carb loading when it is about to run a marathon, right? Well. You are on a very long marathon. (Sugar and caffeine tank and deplete our systems quickly, so *they do not count* as comfort foods. Please limit these.)

A day will come when your body lets you know it's overdue for healthy fruits and veggies. Eventually, I did have to force myself to get enough protein. But give yourself lots of grace until that day comes.

Praise God, my taste buds are coming back! Now, I enjoy things like berries and yogurt, arroz y frijoles, saag and naan, macky-cheese, and pad see ew. Bread and butter. These favorite meals help me perk back up.

Hydration, fresh air, and sunshine.

Pretty obvious, but so necessary.

Exercise.

Bone weary people feel like they can't budge. But moving throughout the day will help increase energy and deepen sleep. It all works together. This doesn't mean run a marathon (unless you *really* want to). It just means walk to the mailbox or stand up and stretch a little. Take up adult ballet, line dancing, or swimming. Even vacuuming counts, if you ask me. Double win.

Sleep.

You know the basics—consistent bedtime, light therapy or sunshine in the morning, exercise, no screens at night, and black out your bedroom (until you can't even see your hand in front of your face.) But also, anoint your home and bedroom. At night, experiment with taking magnesium, rubbing magnesium lotion on your neck, and putting cedarwood, lavender, or other calming essential oils on the bottom of your feet. Play instrumental hymns or scriptural lullabies like "Hidden in My Heart," try gratitude journaling for mental health, and pray as you lie down in bed. Imagine yourself giving every concern that comes to God for safekeeping while you rest. But even if you do everything "right," sleep can be elusive. So then we lean into the Lord. Resting your body and praying in the dark is still more restorative than scrolling on a screen.

Lower expectations.

I grew up in a hippie culture where we recycled, reduced, reused. We even sang about it. Allowing myself a break from those rules and investing in paper plates felt rebellious but necessary. I reminded myself that this is only for a season.

Dan and I were foodies and frugal, making everything from scratch. But I had to lower expectations, accepting the extra cost of frozen or boxed meals because at least there would be food. This is only for a season.

Listen to your body.

Take mental health days for you and your kids. Journal, pray, lie down. Don't worry about running late or canceling plans last minute. Be honest with people when you RSVP, giving yourself an out; if not an "I can't," then an "I'd love to come, but please understand that I may have to back out last minute if a grief wave hits me."

There's nothing revolutionary about self-care. You know what to do. The trick is in the *doing*. That's why becoming aware of your particular signs of "wilting" is key. It's like a gauge to help you know when you need more Vitamin D, hydration, mashed potatoes, or thanksgiving.

For me, signs of wilting include irritability (from too much stress and not enough rest or life-giving activities) and circles under my eyes (from either not getting to bed early enough or not eating the right foods).

Pay attention this week. What are *your* signs of wilting? Also notice the signs of wilting for those you look after.

What foods or liquids sound comforting *and* healing to you right now?

What's *one* self-care practice you will focus on *actually* doing the next couple weeks?

Lord, You take good care of me. Tend to me.
Minister to me. Help me take good care of myself
and those I look after too.

ISAIAH 40:8 • PSALM 3:3 • MATTHEW 11:28–30

horses and healing

I have a healthy fear and appreciation of horses, like I do of the ocean. Majestic and massive, but I'm fine appreciating both from a safe distance. Don't want to get in too deep. I don't want to get bucked off or stepped on either. But since my girls love horses, I was happy to accept an invitation from a merciful woman to visit the barn and meet her horse, Jack.

As I put my hand on Jack's nose, his whole demeanor changed. He closed his eyes and bowed his head, clearly in reverence and mercy for the pain I carried. The moment he closed his eyes, I burst into tears. I thought I was fine, but my smile did not fool him. His tenderness and knowing caught me off guard. (Jack means "God is gracious." He sure is.)

New in town, I was used to people not knowing my story, not caring, and not asking. But as I stood in that freezing barn in winter, the Holy Spirit drew near through a gentle giant. It did something to me.

I felt seen.

The barn was so cold I could see my breath and how shallow my breathing had become. No wonder I felt hollow. The woman who owned Jack taught me a grounding exercise. She told me to close my eyes and let my breath rise and fall deeply with my arms wrapped around Jack's middle like a hug. He was huge, strong, solid. And warm. With my arms wrapped around his body, those deep breaths forced my shallow fight-or-flight breathing to slow down and deepen. It strengthened my atrophied lung capacity and poured security into my heart.

I remembered when we vacationed at the dude ranch, they told me about how their horses know the trails intimately. They trained their horses so well they could carry seven-year-olds with no lead experience through the wilderness of mountain terrain. Their horses could lead wounded warriors through the trails too, veterans without limbs to guide the horses' reigns.

In loss, that's a picture of you and me. We've got no lead experience and nothing left to take the reins. All we've got are deep breaths and trust that grace will lead the way.

Back at the freezing barn, I swung a leg over the saddle. I noticed how we began to move together. My spine swayed a bit with his. The horse's rhythm seemed to reset neuropathways inside of me. Shaking down some trauma on a micro-level that I can't explain. When I feel hopeless or limp, I remember that grace will lead the way.

Jack taught me that healing can be unearthed in the most unusual places.

> Socially acceptable coping doesn't always equal healthy coping.

The rhythm of a horse. The purr of a kitten. The breath of a puppy. (Pet stores often let you hold puppies if you ask real sweet.) Snuggling a teddy bear, a pillow, or a warm pack can offer comfort too, even to a grown man. Ain't no shame, and nobody has to know.

Jack also taught me that trying something new is a good coping strategy. Some who grieve pick up baking or renovation projects. Knitting. Hiking. Retail therapy. Binge watching a good Jane Austen series. Painting. Dancing. Running. A new job.

However, socially acceptable coping doesn't always equal healthy coping. Running or retail therapy can slip from a coping mechanism to an addiction. (I think anything can.) Overworking might be praised by your boss, but is it healthy? If workaholism becomes a struggle for you, pray God will help you put healthy boundaries around your work hours. (You can pray for healthy boundaries around anything you need help managing.)

All coping has merit, but within healthy moderation, right? Is excess when it becomes unhealthy? I can't tell you if your coping is healthy or not. These are honest questions and boundaries you'll need to take before the Lord. The Holy Spirit will guide you. Just do yourself a favor, and be teachable with open ears and a humble heart. And remember what we talked about in Grief 101: the boundary line around grief is love.

What I can tell you with certainty is that God gives us breath, our primary regulator and beautifully designed coping mechanism. When we panic, we've literally held our breath. I can tell you that in Him, we live and move and have our being.[1] Sometimes deep breath is deep prayer.

Take four deep breaths in through your nose and out through your mouth. As your chest rises and then falls, pray, "Holy Spirit, come." What do you notice?

Describe a moment or a time when you felt seen:

Brainstorm a few ways you're coping lately plus some new ones you want to try:

Are you coping in ways that are not good for your body or heart?

Breath of Life, every cell in my body needs You.
Fill these hollow places with new strength and security.
Would you send me a good healing hug (and
maybe some puppies to hold)? Quiet me with your love.
Don't let my hands hang limp. Instead give me
courage to follow where You lead. Show me the paths
that lead to life and give me strength to close off
paths that lead to destruction. Lord, give me healthy
coping mechanisms. Break off soul ties and bondage
to unhealthy ways of coping. Set me free.

1 CORINTHIANS 13:4–13 • JOHN 20:22 • ACTS 17:22–23

blessings, bittersweet

They say to count your blessings. Well . . . somedays, I'm too tired to count. And most blessings feel bittersweet right now anyway.

The Bible asks, "Where, O death, is your sting?"[1] I get that this verse refers to how believers are free from the sting of sin after we die. But when I hear, "Death, where is your sting?" all I can think is that it stings right here, deeply, all over my body. The grace I guess is that is the sting is not an eternal affliction for the believer; it's momentary.[2] Every little joy stings because I can't share it with Dan. Every celebration has a sliver of sorrow.

I've heard the verses that say that joy will come after sorrow but have no desire to entertain this. Maybe desire is the wrong word. Maybe I just have no strength or bandwidth or margin to even think about joy coming after sorrow. I welcome joy when it surprises me in quiet blessings and loud ones, full of laughter. I receive those bits of joy that hold the hand of sorrow. But I want nothing to do with *just* joy. I feel loyal to my sorrow and refuse to leave it behind. At least today, anyway.

When I held a baby for the first time after Dan died, the celebration of life crashed in with the sorrow of his absence. Maybe sorrow will always be a little black balloon that will, from here on out, be mixed in with every bouquet of wedding flowers, newborn showers, and birthday festivities. Maybe I can muster up some thanksgiving even if there's sorrow mixed in.

Gratitude has saved me from depression and unhealthy thought-cycles in the past. It's a powerful tool in my back pocket that I sometimes forget to use. Gratitude has the power to cut through heaviness and oppressive fog.

But there's something healthy about acknowledging what is going poorly too. I sit down to record a list of blessings, but also blessings that feel bittersweet. Then I give myself permission to write what's just hard, where I don't see blessing in it at all. This feels authentic to my soul. I'm not going to sugarcoat the enormity of the loss and trauma. But I do need to train my eyes to see that, even in the darkest valley, light still pierces through.

I count you, every blessing—
the gift of a fresh haircut
because saggy eyes and a bad haircut . . .
it's a little much.
I thank God for the anonymous giver
and the chance to look and feel refreshed.

I count you, every blessing also bittersweet—
I weep as she washes my hair in the sink,
remembering how you dried my hair
when I was too weak.

Swishing my new hairdo
in the sun and fall breeze—
leaves me wishing for your hands
combing through,
leaves me wishing for the band
on your wedding finger.
How my eyes close and heart swells and I linger
in that moment
when you touch me.

So I ache all the more, and I weep—
I count you every blessing, bittersweet.

◆

Now, it's your turn to find some light in the darkness.

blessings	blessings, bittersweet	just plain hard

Father, help us see the joy mixed into our sorrow.
Help us see provision in the middle of the abandonment
and isolation. Lord, help me remember that every good
gift comes from You. Thank You for these blessings and
for the blessings, bittersweet. For the rest of it that's
just hard, cover it with comfort and peace.

JAMES 1:17 · PSALM 100:4–5 · LUKE 1:76–79

junkyards and redemption

With our wedding anniversary coming up, getting my toes done or going out for a nice dinner didn't feel right. Not even a massage. I knew those celebrations might make me feel Dan's absence even worse. All that came to mind this time was to do something crazy I've never done before. I wanted to see the junkyard. Judging by the curiously wide smile on my face, I decided this idea must be divinely inspired.

If searching for any trace of redemption, the junkyard seemed like an appropriate, promising place to look.

But driving myself was not going to happen. I knew Samwise would be a safe person to ask for a ride. He doesn't try to fix my problems; he just lets me know I'm not alone as I face them. He agreed to take me and said he needed to find a part for his Jeep anyway. I didn't know where the junkyard was, so it felt a little surreal when we drove right by the military base where Dan and I were married twelve years prior, right about the time we were saying our vows of "to have and to hold . . . in sickness and health . . . till death do us part" and kissing at the altar. Twelve years later, instead of my wedding dress, I wore my grandpa's old flannel shirt like a security blanket. But a little joy cut through the swirl of sorrow and memory. Anticipation began to build like a song. *I am going to the junkyard, looking for redemption!*

This was the first week of lockdown. Grocery stores were abuzz,

full of panicking people and empty shelves. But it was peaceful at
the junkyard. Folks were friendly, unhurried, and calm.

I found a crinkled bumper sticker on an old Ford truck that
spoke volumes: "If you're walking through hell, keep going."

Noted.

I sat on an old tire to read a text message from one of the guys
Dan and I had taken in as our own. I hadn't heard from this young
man since the funeral, so the timing and the kindness in his words
struck a chord. I felt remembered. Dan felt remembered. And I
just wept.

Then I learned that we entrust our entire lives to emergency
brakes every single day. Samwise pulled one out of an old Jeep
with strong, oil-stained hands and some plyers. To my surprise,
emergency brakes are just tiny springs and a tiny square of metal,
unseen. Maybe we all have more faith and trust than we know,
buried down deep within us?

Being here reminds me of my great-grandpa, a glorious
dumpster diver who taught me how to find gold buried in gar-
bage cans and alleyways—a life-lesson we all must learn. Redemption is only found where broken pieces lay. And hope is
assembled in suffering.

While we pick up broken pieces and assemble hope in the day-
to-day, we sometimes notice our healing or hurting most when
we hit a milestone on the calendar. Every anniversary, holiday,
birthday, or "first" without our loved one is a new "grief milestone" in our journey.

Milestones can be celebrated, avoided, or survived. There's no
wrong answer. Grief often turns dates that used to be filled with
celebration into dates filled with dread or extra pain. Some people feel weighty expectations to honor their loved ones at every
anniversary, but I can't keep that pace. So, I treat each milestone

differently, asking myself and my kids, "Do we want to celebrate this holiday or birthday?" I ask myself if I want to acknowledge the "death-a-versary" each year. Or do we need to just get through it? Sometimes just "pretending" it's a normal day is all we can handle. Sometimes, we want to do something special. Like visiting the junkyard on my anniversary. It felt like celebrating the wonder and adventure Dan and I cultivated in our marriage in a way that didn't rub salt into the wound.

For Dan's birthday, we watch a movie and enjoy his favorite dessert: chocolate and peanut butter anything. One year, we videotaped a favorite memory about Daddy. Another year, we wrote prayers and notes on balloons and sent them up toward heaven. For me, the release is the most powerful part of a sorrowful remembrance like this. After we've poured our hearts out to the Deliverer, we have to physically let go.

I have noticed a typical pattern for how I handle holidays and special occasions. Days leading up are full of low-grade dread and holding my breath in anticipation. Usually, the big day holds surprising moments of great joy coupled with a surge of dammed up tears. We're lifted on a cloud of the prayers of the people. But in the days after, I think prayers lessen. I think the body can't keep holding its breath. And I think the balloons pop. For days after, I lie flat on a couch.

Noticing a pattern helps you handle future milestones. Helps you get low and ride the waves better. I learned to not schedule anything in the weeks after an important first or milestone, giving white space for potential fallout.

And then there's the waves you can't prepare for. For me, the death-a-versary came with unexpected torrents of PTSD. Dan was missing for six days, so reliving the week he went missing requires great endurance. I couldn't even talk about this one with my children, but our bodies sure remembered. Waking up crying, debilitating flashbacks, paralyzing nightmares. I don't share that to scare you, but to console you. Because I wish I understood what was happening. I would've been able to communicate with those around me better and could've protected my heart better. I would've chosen solitude over surprises. The best thing we did was go painting with a friend—an individual, quiet, expressive activity where I wasn't alone in the room. Then we got ice cream.

Expect that some of these times will be filled with surprising joy and others might be harder than you anticipate. Take heart. This is normal. Ask your prayer team to pray in advance. Plan something you'll look forward to (manicure, bubble bath, batting cages, putt-putt, a new book, dumpster diving). Give yourself freedom to back out if you need to. Listen to your gut. Carefully consider the people you want around you that day. Someone who's funny, sensitive, wise, or prayerful?

Remember you could experience an emotional hangover, so don't over-schedule the days that follow. Create room to breathe and recover.

While some of these milestones, "firsts," and anniversaries may be even harder than your day-to-day, others will mark the calendar with a special occasion to treasure-hunt for comforting memories and dumpster dive to create new ones.

———— ◆ ————

Do you notice a pattern for how you lead up to anniversaries and holidays? How do you handle the day-of and the week after?

Brainstorm activities, people, or places that might feel comforting:

Brainstorm activities, places, and people you need to avoid:

anniversaries, firsts, holidays coming up:	Ideas for what to do:	What not to do / what to avoid:
●		
○		
○		
●		

God who goes before me, as another big milestone
approaches, please walk ahead of me and plan
that day. Give me courage to plan and freedom to
change plans if I need to. Help me listen to Your
Holy Spirit and to my body. Leave treasures for me to
find in the middle of all this junk. Put the community
or the solitude I need in place. Hold me together on that
big day, in the days leading up to it, and the days
that follow. You can redeem anything, so I give You my
broken pieces and ask You to create a beautiful
new thing out of these ashes. Give me eyes to see the
ways You make everything new, even my life.

ECCLESIASTES 3:11 • ROMANS 15:13 • ISAIAH 43:19 • PHILIPPIANS 3:7–11

PART FOUR

COMPANIONS IN SORROW

(grief + community)

when they pass the baton

Some people just don't know how to enter in. So they just don't. Other than the exhaustion and physical pain of sorrow, it's the isolation that really kills me. I often felt like the man in the story of the Good Samaritan who was robbed, beat up, and left for dead on the side of the highway, while many passed by and hurried along or looked the other way. What I thought were life-long, thick-or-thin friendships became strained and people drifted. In addition to losing Dan, I felt like I lost everybody. Seems the heart is easily bruised when it's already been broken.

Thank goodness for a few good Samaritans who came alongside to care for me. Without them, I doubt I would've made it.

Our military family has shared life in close communities, much like the kind described in Acts 2. We cooked for each other, raised each other's kids, provided whatever anyone needed, and did each other's dishes and laundry. Now when I need that the most, I feel like it's me and crickets.

But there are also people who don't know how to enter in and they brave it anyway.

I often remember Rosalinda's words, "The people I thought would show up for us, they didn't. But I was completely surprised by the people who did." She said her entire support system changed.

She helps me feel less targeted and abnormal. Most widows I

meet feel a deep level of isolation, and we think we're the only ones to feel that way (which feels even more isolating). Moms who lost a child tell me their friends don't get them anymore. Widowers who used to have steady double dates with couple-friends aren't invited anymore. It happened to Job, David, and Jesus too. Abandoned, avoided, or rejected in our loss.

Losing our familiar support people is another loss to grieve, compounding the heartache. Sometimes a spirit of isolation sneaks in through the back door of loss and tells you nobody cares. Hear me right now. That's a lie. *A believable lie that feels very true. But it's not truth.*

I care. And there are people in your life who care, deeply. They just might be different people than those we expected would step in. That's the key right there.

In general, folks want to help and often just feel helpless to know how, whether these are friends, organizations, or church groups. Whether virtual or in real life, long-distance or local. Some may avoid us, but there are others we can lean on in our time of need. Sometimes, those we thought would be there for us love us so deeply and feel so helpless that they're immobilized themselves. Because they're grieving too. They lost your person too. And they lost the person you used to be. This is hard for everyone.

But with hindsight (and after hours of sobbing, feeling left for dead, and crying out to God), a revelation slowly unfolds. Instead of losing my support network, I wonder if it's a passing of the baton instead. God knew who could get us this far, and He also knows who is equipped to take us the next leg of the journey.

Dan and I hardly watched TV, but when we did, we loved us some "Fixer Upper." While Chip Gaines, co-host of the DIY show, excels at demo and reconstruction, his wife Jo specializes in the rebuilding and the making of a home. Both are mission critical, but Chip just can't do what Jo can do (though he tries). And I can't imagine Joanna throwing herself through a wall the way Chip does. There's always a key moment when Chip completes his mission and passes the baton (in the form of a rake, a shovel, or a shoe) to Joanna. I've come to believe the loss of a loved one is a long series of passing the baton.

The reality is that Dan is the one I miss most, and no one can fill his shoes. But other torch bearers can carry on the relay, right? I imagine Jesus taking the light from Dan's torch and passing on the flame to other appointed and anointed relay racers. Some carry candles, sparklers, lanterns. Maybe even torches.

We may not recognize the people who do want to step in when we keep wanting our old people to step up. *Make new friends and keep the old, right?*[1] Well, now's the time, I guess.

Instead of focusing on who else I lost, I try to remember who I've gained. I'm not saying that's easy. But I thank God for the handful of people He did bring into my life. They truly are uniquely qualified to be trust-builders, comforters, and helpers.

The image of passing the baton comforts me and gives me hope for who might come into our lives next. It helps us release the people who aren't willing or equipped for this leg of the journey and helps us appreciate the new people who are.

⸻ ◆ ⸻

What are some of the roles the loved one you lost used to fill in your life? (For example, Dan was my best friend, prayer partner, accountant, lawn mower . . .)

Do you feel like you lost other relationships when you lost your loved one? Have you felt avoided, rejected, or abandoned? It's good to write about it.

Who are the people who have stepped up and stepped in? Who have you gained in your life?

Write the names of people and organizations who you feel let you down. Pray: *Father, I choose to forgive them. I release them to You.*

Father, I miss vibrant community and having a companion who knows me fully. Uproot isolation, rejection, and abandonment from my heart. I break off any agreements and alliances I've made with these things. I'm not an orphan; You've adopted me as Your own. Help me process the changing roles in my community. Help me release the people who need to step out of my life now. Please bring anointed and willing people into my life to get me through the season ahead.

JOB 19:14 • PSALM 38:9–11 • ISAIAH 53:4 • ISAIAH 40:1

build an emotional support team

I've hiked weeklong fourteener trips, but grief is the hardest range I've ever climbed. When you go on long treks, especially to places like Everest or the Inca Trail, you really can't go alone. You have to work as a team. Along this grief journey, I've identified about seven supportive types of companions in sorrow.

Guides see the big picture. They're familiar with the route, helping the group summit breathtaking views and avoid risks and danger along the way. They keep tabs on everyone and check on morale. They appoint the lead and the sweeper. They distribute food, gear, and weight appropriately. Guides also help prioritize what to carry in your pack and what to leave behind. If you're wise, take counsel.

Leads walk the road ahead of us. They've experienced similar loss. Leads listen. They help us pace ourselves. They've learned lessons the hard way, so their wisdom is a safety net and guide-post. (Rosalinda is a perfect example of a lead in my story.) Leads have already weathered storms that are just beginning to brew in our lives. But somehow, they made it through. Witnessing their strength and stability gives us hope. If you're wise, be teachable.

Walking partners keep good company as we move forward and take breathers together. We honor each other's losses with presence, questions, and listening ears. We put our arms around each other's shoulders when we get hurt. Some excel at swapping war stories. Some go there to make us laugh. Others help you appreciate the beautiful landscape instead of staring at your boots. (Samwise is a great example.)

Porters or Sherpas shoulder the heavy weights of emotional burdens and/or prayer. They're acclimated to the high elevations and are experienced and strong. If you're wise, you won't stuff your emotions and try to carry all the burden yourself. (Erika, my prayer partner, is a great example of this.)

Stragglers are those who just got started on the trail. They're not acclimated, and they're getting blisters because their new hiking boots aren't broken in yet. They don't think they're going to make it. We've all been there. We may only have a few more steps on the trail than they do, but our job is to look out for them.

Grief sometimes tricks you into thinking you don't have to care for others. Sometimes, you'll be carried. Other times, you'll carry someone else, even with your injury, limp, and broken heart. The comfort and wisdom passed down to us, we pass down to others. Because the whole hike doesn't revolve around us. And that's good news!

Sweepers are always the very last person on the trail. When you feel like you mentally, physically, or spiritually cannot make it, you will never drop behind a sweeper in your life. (Dan was always the sweeper.) Fit and capable, they take the rear to encourage, refresh, and pray us stragglers forward. They'll ensure you never walk alone. Even if you feel like you don't have a sweeper on earth, Jesus is always sweeping, leaving the ninety-nine to find the one who can't keep up.

In a big hiking group, mini-groups will walk together. All these mini-groups have to stay within range of each other enough to hear or see the group ahead of you and the group behind you. When hiking in a group, communication is key. Never assume someone's okay just because you haven't heard from them in a while. Usually, the worse an injury, the less ability someone has to call for help. That's why we keep tabs, check in, and keep communication lines open. The lead makes sure they're going at a pace everyone can follow and the sweeper makes sure no one is left behind or struggles alone.

While group hiking doesn't have a cheer section on the sidelines, I'm breaking from the analogy to add these mission critical companions.

Your cheering section is made up of those who can't relate to your pain, but they can hydrate and nourish you. Their posters say: "You can do it! Look how far you've come! Keep going!" They cook you marathon pasta, watch your kids, and generally hold down the fort while you trek on. They believe in you and marvel at your strength and endurance.

That's about all of us.

With affection, I call this motley crew of companions in sorrow the Fellowship of the Brokenhearted.

While we need each other, sometimes we don't get to have all the companions we wish we had for the journey. When I feel like I'm lacking, I remember that the Holy Spirit takes on each and every single one of these roles. He goes before us and behind us. He encourages, counsels, and nourishes us. He weeps, laughs, and takes five with us. The Holy Spirit is our lead and sweeper, porter and walking partner, our guide and friend.

———— ◆◆◆ ————

What are some ways you can see the Holy Spirit filling these companion roles?

Who is filling any of these roles in your life? One person may fill a lot of these. And some people you thought might fill these roles but can't or won't. Ask God for eyes to see who might be willing but you haven't let them in yet.

Guides (pastors, mentors, counselors)

Leads (grief mentors or friends)

Walking partners (listeners, prayer partners, funny friends, huggers, criers, askers of good questions)

Porters or Sherpas (burden carriers, prayer partners, or emotionally intelligent friends)

Stragglers (fellow grievers who you pray for and care for)

Sweepers (those who make sure you never walk alone)

Cheering section (those who encourage and care for you)

Are you longing for any of these roles to be filled in particular? Who can you seek out or invite into your life?

What do you wish you could tell the people around you about your grief process? What if you actually communicated those things to your people?

Lord, lead me into relationships that are mutually life-giving and fulfilling. Show me who I can ask to become my prayer partner and who can be a good listener. Bring the right people into my life. And when there are gaps, thank You for being the God who fills the gaps. In Jesus' name, amen.

PROVERBS 13:20 • 1 CORINTHIANS 15:33–34

when Jesus is your only friend

We become who we hang out with.

My youth pastor taught me that. Pastors often say look at your friends, and that'll be you in five years. We all know we need to choose our friends wisely, and it's especially true now. In a time of loss, identities, personalities, and communities are all changing. We're vulnerable from grief brain and trauma. We've got to be careful who we spend time with in this reshaping season. So if our entire support network is shaken, let's rebuild wisely.

We become who we hang out with.

Yes, be wise in selecting leads and sweepers and hiking buddies. But, also be wise to note who you do *not* want traveling with you. A wise mentor told me that you have to redefine friendships when people demonstrate they're not safe or not equipped to walk with you anymore.

Red flags of unhealthy relationships might be people who are draining, demanding, crossing boundaries, taking advantage, shaming, blaming, and condemning. Also steer clear of the suck-it-uppers.

You may need to avoid certain people temporarily. But you'll also need to identify toxic relationships in your life and cut those ties permanently, as graciously as possible. When you're already in ruins, why invite landmines into your territory?

However, there's a difference between being careful about who you let influence you and isolating yourself. Some who grieve shut the whole world out on purpose and don't allow others in. If that's you, I wonder if you could ask the Lord why you isolate yourself? Fear, anxiety, or self-protection?

I was on the opposite end of the spectrum, desperately looking for community and feeling pushed away by others. Sometimes I wonder if that season of forced isolation was a protection, a form of hiddenness, keeping me from additional hurtful situations. It's possible that what I suffered as isolation was the gift of solitude. If only I could've embraced that sooner. It may have saved me from additional heartache. On long journeys, solitude is an invaluable respite.

No matter how amazing your support teams are or no matter how lacking, there may be a time when solitude or isolation usher you into a solo trek on the mountain, when it's just you and only you. I went from being fully known in marriage to feeling fully alone in loss. Carrying burdens unspeakable. All I wanted was for someone to understand everything I carried.

Grief can be an isolating season—whether we feel isolated by others or whether we isolate ourselves. Regardless, at the end of the day, some people will fall short of our expectations and fail us when we need them most. In those times, there's grace and forgiveness. But there's also Jesus.

If we become who we hang out with, I choose Jesus.

Sometimes, Jesus is our only friend. He's the only one who gets us. He's the only one who understands everything we've been through. And He's the only one who gave up His last breath just to save us.

Even in isolation and abandonment, when your relationships are shaken, Jesus remains, and His love for you is unshakable. If no one else, Jesus understands your grief and afflictions and carries them all. If grief is a season of becoming, and if we become who we hang out with, I choose Jesus.

If you you're going to turn out like your friends in five years, how does that settle with you?

Who are people you need to distance from right now?

And which relationships do you need to pursue?

Do you feel isolated by others or are you isolating yourself? Ask the Lord to give you a fresh perspective on the matter.

Lord, give me courage to let go of the relationships
that aren't healthy for me and my children.
Help me choose my companions wisely. In this time,
help me become better friends with You.

PROVERBS 13:20 • 1 CORINTHIANS 15:33–34 • ISAIAH 54:10

JOHN 15:15

when they say dumb things

People who speak well into our suffering often have experienced it themselves. But many people seem to avoid listening to the bereaved by talking *at* them.

Sometimes, people try to show sympathy: "Well, have the best Christmas you can," or "I'm sure this is a horrible birthday for you." Inside, I'm like, *Really?* I'm trying to hold on to hope as best I can here, and I can't handle any outside negativity. *(Danita, they're trying.)*

Merry Christmas. Happy birthday. This is what I love about you . . . I'll never turn that down! But I think people are afraid to say "merry" and "happy" to a grieving person. Makes sense. When Christmas or birthdays roll around, and people simply remind me that they love me, that they're there for me, that they're thinking of me . . . these are cases when it's truly the thought that counts.

And then there's the flat-out condemning or bullying things people say. We remember these words vividly, don't we? You could probably write a list. And maybe you should, just to get it out.

my hurtful things people say list:

o

o

o

After hearing the lists of others, I often think, "Are you kidding me? What were people thinking?"

It's easy to work ourselves into a hissy fit. Especially when the people who said these things are in authority over you, administratively or in the church.

We may even be tempted to transfer people's hurtful actions and words onto how we think of God. I know I did. Even with a solid foundation of God's kindness and faithfulness to me, I still did. The church and authorities are called to represent the heart of the Bridegroom and of the King. That's why our heart's cry is that things would function "on earth as it is in heaven."[1] However, we all fall short, don't we?

Love is patient and love is kind. But *nothing* about the hurtful words people say are loving or kind. I have no doubt these words break God's heart all over again for us. I bet some of them make Him mad too.

In the beginning, I was vigilant about *not* camping out in the ashes of hurtful words. I was vigilant about speaking life over my family and not allowing negativity to get a foothold. But after continual sucker punches and letdowns, that's when bitterness, rejection, or victimization can slip in the back door of our exhaustion. They sneak in quietly when we're too tired and too devastated to even notice or to even care.

So, let's try to sort this out in a safe place. Then we're prepared to respond graciously, with God's help, the next time.

Forgiveness is mission critical.

If we don't continually forgive such hurtful words (and people), then we'll actually remain stuck in bondage *to* them. Forgiveness sets us free *from* them. We can either flex our muscles in forgiveness, or we can let bitterness and victimization begin to take hold of us. It's an either/or.

Forgiveness is not saying it was okay.

It was *not* okay. Forgiveness just takes you out of the judge's seat and removes the gavel from your hand. It gets you out of the way and trusts God to judge the situation.

Forgiveness is not reconciliation.

If someone continues to hurt you until you're no longer emotionally safe around them, distance yourself. Doesn't have to be forever but definitely for now. Whether you mark these people safe or not, you'll need to forgive them regardless.

Forgiveness is not usually a one-and-done either.

Most cannot just "forgive and forget." Usually, hurtful memories get triggered and resurface, and we feel the pain all over again. When this happens, choose to forgive it all over again. This allows us to forgive in deepening layers. With time and diligence, a day will come when you are fully set free, fully healed, and no longer feel the sting. That's why Jesus tells us to forgive not seven times, but seven times seventy.[2] He means to forgive multiple, multiple times until it's complete. Often, we have to be honest with God about how we need His help in this process.

It's devastating—all the hurtful things people say to those who are already hurting. The list is long and could be its own book. I want to confess on behalf of the people who have hurt you, that I am so sorry:

We never should have said those unkind, callous, thoughtless things. Please forgive us. For when we minimized your pain, misunderstood you, avoided you, and rushed you. I'm sorry. When we did not represent the gracious, present, comforting heart of the Father for you. I'm so sorry. On behalf of authorities, I'm so sorry when we did not step in to protect you and support you. And on behalf of the church, I'm sorry for when we did not represent the safe, loving, accepting arms of the family of Christ. When we abandoned you when you needed us the most. When we twisted God's words into weapons. I'm so deeply sorry. When we did not represent the kindness of Jesus to you. Please forgive us.

Let's just sit in that for a moment. Can you offer forgiveness over the hurtful things people have said and done? With a prayer and a red pen, go over each statement on your "hurtful things list" and mark them forgiven in your heart and on paper. Ask God to help you forgive because you likely can't do that in your own strength.

Then, grab your red pen and write a statement that's true and comforting next to each hurtful statement in your list above.

On the other hand, can you remember anything someone said that made you feel seen or comforted? Let's not forget the good stuff.

Anytime something resurfaces that you need to forgive, here's a simple liturgy to read out loud.

A Liturgy of Forgiveness

Lord, here's the hurtful memory again.

I don't know how to forgive.

I don't feel like forgiving.

I can't seem to do it on my own.

But by the power of Jesus,

I choose to forgive it all over again.

I declare it's forgiven. It's in Your hands now.

God of mercy, people said some insensitive
things and some heart-wrenching things. Have mercy
on me. I ask for strength to forgive what feels
unforgivable. Over and over. Remind me of the people
who do care deeply. Remind me of words that do
comfort me. In Jesus' name, amen.

MATTHEW 18:22 · MATTHEW 18:21–35 · MATTHEW 6:12

build a prayer team

You know those moments where you feel like you should be drowning but, somehow, you're not going under? There's a stamina and a peace you can't explain. I call these moments "walking on water." This is 100 percent because God is gracious and because someone is praying for you.

Some days, we can almost tangibly feel the prayers of the people.

When my husband went missing, I immediately started a text thread to reach out to the praying people I know.

I've kept that thread, letting people know how to pray us through some troublesome waters.

I've been very candid with my group. Sometimes, I offer a lament. *Where are you God? How long, O God?* Other times, I offer a praise. *Here's how God came through!* Most often, I just give them specific ways to pray.

I encourage and thank them for their prayers often. (Because I don't want them to give up!) I let them know when God answered, moved quickly, healed or provided like we asked. It builds up our faith and our morale.

Every now and then, I make sure to say, "Feel free to mute this text conversation, or let me know if you need to be taken off the list. I understand that we all have different prayer assignments at different times." I want people to feel like they can bow out if they need to, and I don't take it personally if they do. But most stayed with me.

I will likely continue that text thread for years. Why? Because their prayers have kept me alive.

When you ask for prayer, you are *not* bugging your people. They may even thank you for sending specific prayer requests. They *want* to know how to pray for you and support you. Often, our loved ones feel helpless to know what to do, say, or pray. So offering direction in prayer is a huge relief to them . . . and a huge relief for us to know that these people have our backs.

Today, let's enlist a prayer team for you. Just think of who you trust. You don't need a thousand. It can be two or ten: "For where two or three are gathered together in My name, I am there in the midst of them."[1]

First, consider if you want this to be email, text, etc. Switching to email might've been a good idea since I write such long texts. But when I have the most to say, I send a simple, desperate "SOS."

Second, recruit your prayer warriors. If you can't find the words to get started, just copy this and send it to some praying people: "Hope this finds you well. I'm looking for people who are willing to pray for me in the days ahead as I navigate my loss. I'll just send prayer requests as needed. Let me know if I can include you. Thank you!"

Third, be strategic in your requests. Sometimes, you'll have prayer requests that are too intimate for a larger group. If it's about one of your children, think, "Who do I know that's passionate about praying for my children?" If it's about finances, think, "Who do I know is prayerful *and* good at finances?"

Fourth, there's a difference in asking for advice and asking for prayer, and sometimes you'll need to set that boundary line.

The fifth tip to cover yourself in prayer may surprise you. As people are praying for you, think to yourself, "Who else is grieving that *I* can pray for?" Even when I felt helpless to know what to pray for myself and my children, I felt especially capable to know how to pray for the needs of a fellow widower with young kids. After pouring my heart out in prayer for him and his children, I often added a wonder-working, powerful afterthought to my prayers for their family, "And Lord, would you do that for us too?"

At the end of the day, whether you gather a team or not, I'm in awe that there's always someone who is constantly praying for you. Sometimes, so deeply, it's like He's groaning in agony on your behalf. The Holy Spirit does that for you. Night and day. Father God Himself wrote the prayer, "The LORD bless you and keep you; the LORD make his face shine upon you and be gracious to you."[2] Jesus' prayers for you in the garden are still being answered to this day. Take comfort and thank God for His prayers over you.

◆

Who can you invite to be on your prayer list? Who will be faithful to pray and keep it confidential?

Will you use email? Text? Something else?

Write down the names of the people who agree to join you in prayer. And thank God for them.

Who will you commit to praying for? Shoot them a quick text with a short prayer. For example:

"Lord, I pray for my friend. Hold her, and hold her together."

"Father, I'm grieving alongside my friend today. Thank You for drawing close to the brokenhearted. Draw close to my friend."

Father, please lead me to people who would love to know how to pray for me. Please help me get over this self-conscious guilt I have, like my prayer requests might be a burden or inconvenience to others. Give me courage to ask for the prayer backing that I desperately need. Thank You for the people who are praying for me that I don't even know about. And thank You for Your prayers for me, so my faith won't fail me and so I won't lose heart.

NUMBERS 6:22–27 • JOHN 17:13–24 • ROMANS 8:26–27 • LUKE 18:1–8 *when they ask how you're doing*

Someone asked how I'm doing today. Makes me realize how many people never actually ask me that. I think they're afraid of my answers or they're afraid it's a stupid question. I was glad my friend was brave enough to ask.

I want to tell my friend that I'm still pretty up and down. That I'm surprised how much I still laugh. That I cried myself to sleep thinking about Dan missing the children's winter choir concert. How he was the perfect man for me, and I still have a hard time believing he's not coming back. How I keep his root beer in the fridge, ready for him to walk in the door. Should be any day now. How it hurts when days upon days go by where no one checks in to ask how I'm doing.

"How are you doing, friend?" is such a difficult question to answer. Some days, I just say, "This is hard. It's harder than hard." Other days, I say, "There is grace when you walk through fire." Sometimes, I just say, "I don't really know." There's a grace given to you for exactly how you are doing. Even without the ability to express how we're doing, there is a grace for it.

———— ◆ ————

Do you sometimes dread this question? Do you also sometimes wish someone would just be brave enough to ask you how you're doing?

How do you respond when people ask you, "How are you doing?"

How would you *like* to respond when they ask you?

Father, we receive Your grace today.
And we ask You for more of it. You know how we're
really doing, and You know what we really need.
Lord, keep Your word. You promise that those who fear
You lack no good thing.[1] Provide my every emotional,
spiritual, physical, hormonal, relational, financial,
mental, and communal need. I need grace to lead
me today. In Jesus' name, amen.

PSALM 34:9 • ROMANS 9:16 • EPHESIANS 2:4–10

build a practical help team

When you first lose your person and you're stunned and shocked, that's when people most frequently ask, "What do you need?" I didn't know the answer. The question overwhelmed me. All I could say was, "I need Dan."

When that clearly annoyed the military officials who apparently didn't expect an honest answer, I started to make up fictitious answers. Even to this day, if people ask what I need, I sometimes whisper, "I need Dan."

But once I got my bearings, the list of what I needed grew impossibly long. That was about the time people tapered off asking. Oh well. And that's when we have to learn to ask others for the help we need.

However, I didn't even know who to ask. I found that when appliances broke, cars died, and plumbing leaked, my brain just went blank. It's kind of paralyzing. In distress, I suddenly felt like I had nobody I could turn to. Dan was my go-to in these situations, so I had to retrain my brain. So the Holy Spirit prompted me to write a list of need-based categories and then name people who could help in those areas if something came up.

Today, we're going to make a list of things you need help with. Keep it on a list-making app or on a note in your wallet. Here's why. When someone who genuinely wants to help you asks,

"What can I do?", instead of saying, "I don't know," you can give a few options from your list.

After I made my list, a woman I met at church asked how she could help, and she genuinely wanted to. Thanks to my handy-dandy list, I answered easily, "I need help driving the dog to the groomer." She was delighted to know a simple way she could take a load off me. Most people are genuinely honored and happy to pitch in when they can. After all, I find great joy and satisfaction helping others when I can. Don't you?

We have to drop the pride and either accept when help is offered or call and ask for it. The worst that can happen is that they say no. I take that back. The *worst* that can happen is when they say they will but don't. But the best thing that can happen is they come help! That's worth asking and risking some no's or false promises. You can also say, "Can you *or someone you know* help me with . . ." That can inspire people to think outside the box. "I can't right now, but my brother-in-law can help you." *Sweet!*

When someone replaced my dead car battery, he responded, "It's easy. No problem." I was dumbfounded. Easy? For the chronically ill or the brokenhearted, what's overwhelming to us is simple for others. That's why we need to share each other's burdens. What weighs a thousand pounds to me may be a feather to someone else. Crisis season won't last forever. But now is the season for leaning on community to get through a rough patch.

Whenever needs arise and my mind goes blank, I refer to my list. At the bottom of my list, I added a reminder, "I am not alone." I taped the list to my wall. Now when I pass by it, whether or not I'm in distress, it counters the lie that no one cares. I see the list of names, smile, and thank God for them, remembering that I'm not alone.

◆

If you could answer with extravagant honesty, without guilt, practicality, or filter, what would you say if asked, "What do you need right now?" Brain-dump anything you need.

Now it's time to write out your list of people you can call on. Reassess and add names as needed. Ask God to highlight people with experience in each category. Challenge categories might include watching the kids, house repairs, car repairs, administration tasks, financial advice, dog sitting, budgeting, and yard work.

Challenges : | people who can help

Now retrace these words, as many times as you need to:

I am not alone.

You are my ever-present help in time of need.
I feel like I buried my loved one, and now I'm buried in
paperwork and responsibilities. Forgive me for pride and
embarrassment keeping me from letting others into my
mess to help. Give me courage to ask for and to accept
help. When people offer, help me know what to ask for.
Forgive me for buying into the lie that I'm abandoned
and alone. Send me uniquely gifted and talented people
for such a time as this. In Jesus' name, amen.

MATTHEW 7:7–8 • PROVERBS 11:25 • PSALM 46:1 • GALATIANS 6:2

PART FIVE

DERAILED AND SHAKEN

(doubts + questions)

permission to ask why

"Why?" It's a question I didn't ask for at least a couple months. People around me kept crying out, "Why? Why? Why?" on my behalf. But not me, and I'm not sure exactly why.

I think I had to focus on the right here and right now problems, or I knew I'd go under too fast. Or maybe I had to just trust God, or I knew I'd go under too fast. Or maybe I was just in too much shock or wasn't brave enough to go there. Likely, it was a combination of all those things.

I don't recommend watching *Sleepless in Seattle* after being widowed. It hit me differently. However, there was one redeeming quote I had to write down. The widower says slowly and thoughtfully, "It isn't fair. There's no reason for it. But if you start asking why, you'll go crazy."[1]

Maybe that's why I couldn't ask why.

It took me weeks before shock wore thin enough for me to even formulate the question. But when I was finally ready to ask it, the question burst out like the breaking of water. "Why?" spilled out of my lips, kind of explosive-like. A constant series of calamities forced the question out of my mouth. It rushed out with a vengeance like pushing during childbirth.

"Why?! Why?! Why?! Why?! Why?!"

Why him? Why now? When we had no home, no community, no church home, no safety net at school, no answers on my writing, no direction, no anchor? Why when we finally got my health back and when we finally had hopes for the future again?

And then I wondered. *Am I allowed to even ask why? Is that okay? Is it useful? Did Jesus ever ask why?*

And then I remembered the cross. Oh, Lord. Oh, my Savior. Yes. Jesus asked why. And He did so in more agony than I'll ever know. In more suffering, darkness, betrayal, and isolation than I'll ever know. He cried out with His last painful breath:

"My God, my God, *why* have you forsaken me?"[2]

His pain was so palpable and powerful that the sky turned dark, the earth shook, the rocks split, and many dead saints were raised to life.[3] And as He breathed His last, the one-foot-thick veil between holiness and humanity tore in two, a tearing like when delivering a child. The cross felt closer to home than ever, as I squatted on the floor of my little apartment bathroom. Groans unexplainable and fierce wailings of "Why, God? Why?" Maybe we won't get answers to our whys, but it sure feels like breakthrough to finally ask. A childlike faith is full of questions, wonders, curiosities and even doubts. Healthy faith knows how to be kind to doubt. But let's agree that there's a difference in questioning God's plan for you and questioning His heart for you. I've questioned all of it before.

> Let's agree that there's a difference in questioning God's plan for you and questioning His heart for you.

Dan and I walked through one of my darkest seasons of questioning God together. I was so chronically ill that I couldn't lift my laundry basket. I didn't sleep, and I was tormented in my soul. *Why?* How could a good God hear our prayers but let me suffer?

Then my pastor gave me permission to doubt God and permission to ask why. I learned that bringing doubts and questions before the Lord is actually an act of faith. *Lord, I believe, help me overcome my unbelief.*[4] It's a humble act that says, "I don't understand, but I know You do. I don't have peace, but I know You can give that to me. I don't feel like trusting You, but I want to."

I wrestled God's goodness and His mercy so fiercely that I almost gave up faith and hope entirely. But thanks to God's goodness and mercy, that was also the season where I learned to trust and surrender like never before. Ooh. *Did you catch that?* My darkest days of doubt were what taught me to trust God the most. May He redeem Your darkest days too.

―――――― ◆◆◆ ――――――

Have you given yourself permission to tell God how you feel? Why or why not?

I've shared some of my whys. When you're ready, list your whys here. (If you have no words, an angry scribble will suffice.)

Shepherd, You gather me into Your arms.
You carry me. When I can't breathe or think, You are
with me. But God, I don't understand. I hate that this
happened. Why? Why didn't You prevent this? Why can't
we go back and change it? Show me where You were
when I needed You the most. Thank You for letting me
ask these things. Thank You for hearing me out, for
weeping alongside me. You comfort me like a mother
comforting her child. When I needed You the most,
You were with me, holding me close.

ISAIAH 40:11 • ISAIAH 66:13 • PSALM 27:13–14

surrendering whys

The same week after I finally braved asking why, I received an email from an old colleague who said he had been asking God why Dan died. And he felt like he got an answer. He believed Dan's death was to increase my ministry. I could tell he felt a solid sense of resolution and was kind of happy about that.

But between you and me, yes, sure. Maybe that's a part of it. *Maybe?* But it's not really an answer to "WHY?!" You can never ever explain and tie up the reason for someone's death with such a neat and tidy bow.

The fact is, God never created us for death. Rosalinda reminds me that death wasn't part of the original design. So it's no surprise that our bodies go into shock and our minds can't comprehend loss and death when we come across it. People don't die because God smites them. People die because of sin, sickness, accidents, hatred, murder, darkness, and on and on. God doesn't cause tragedy or destruction. But in His compassion for us, He does know how to redeem it.

It's dangerous ground to say that *everything* that happens has been planned by God. When we do that, we risk blaming works of the enemy and fallen mankind on a compassionate and holy God. God gave us free will from the beginning because He loves freedom.[1] He wants children who freely love Him, a Bride who freely chooses Him.

Let's not forget that it's the enemy who steals, kills, and destroys.[2] Not the Lord. Jesus came to restore heaven to earth like it was in the garden. He came to redeem all that's been lost and slain and to rebuild all that's been broken and destroyed. Jesus came so that we would have life, abundant life, eternal life.

In forcing an answer, sometimes people say, "Well, it was God's plan." What if it wasn't? What if death was never part of God's original plan? I also hear forced answers like, "Yeah, they told me that my brother had to die so that our cousin could accept Christ." No. Jesus' death is all that is required for salvation. God can bring people to faith without someone else's death. These trite and tidy answers don't reflect God's kind heart for us, do they? And they're hurtful. I'm so sorry if someone ever said anything like that to you.

Thankfully, the very week I finally asked "Why, God? Why?" and the book on asking why arrived and the colleague emailed me with his "answer" to my why, I also received this email:

My Dear Friend Danita,

After I heard about what happened to Dan, I kept asking the Lord: "Why?"

Something similar happened to a close friend of ours a couple of years ago. He also had two little kids. Back then, I kept asking the Lord "Why?" as well. I don't question anymore. I trust. You taught me the real meaning of surrendering to Him . . .

Abraços apertados pra você e para as meninas,

[Big hugs for you and your girls],

Camila

When we demand or force answers to "Why me," tension and unrest follow. But Camila reminds me that surrendering to God and trusting in Him is the quickest path to peace. God fills those who trust in Him with peace and joy.[3] She also helps me see the difference between questioning that's rooted in mistrusting God and the questioning that's honest wrestling with our storylines.

Some of us don't like to live in any tension of the unexplained. We want resolution. So, when we come to a shadow of an answer, we let that give our hearts a false sense of rest. But I know true rest, and true rest is what and who I'm after. True rest comes when we surrender to the Jesus who won't spill all His secrets and won't tell us all our future holds and won't always explain all our whys.

We're not alone in asking our whys. Gideon, Rebekah, David, and even Jesus asked. Some got answers and some didn't. Elisabeth Elliot was a missionary who was widowed two times. I love how she frames God's response to our whys: "The psalmist often questioned God, and so did Job. God did not answer the questions, but he answered the man—with the mystery of himself."[4]

True rest for the weary and bereaved is found when we throw our broken hearts and cares upon Jesus, letting the mystery of who He is be enough. This is the ministry of His presence.

Are there "answers" people have tried to give you to explain your loved one's death?

How did you respond?

How did you really feel about it?

Have you yourself tried to explain the death away? People of faith can super-spiritualize someone's death as a coping mechanism. I did. Have you done that too? Tell me how.

Father, help me trust You when I cannot understand. You invite me to come to You when I'm weary. Here I am, Lord. Give me deep rest. Please let the whys of my heart take a rest today too. I may never make sense of what feels senseless, so today, I'm asking You for peace instead of answers. Heal me from where people have hurt me with trite, tidy bows. Remind me that my loved one's life, legacy, and purpose are too far-reaching and beautiful and eternal to wrap up with a simple answer.

MATTHEW 11:28–29 • JOHN 10:10 • GALATIANS 5:1 • ROMANS 15:13

flipping whys

Big stacks of mail filled my tiny apartment. Mail from the government, banks, family, and friends. I was scared of the numbers and words I might find in those envelopes, so I couldn't open most of it. Not yet anyway.

However, the very day I woke up crying out "Why?! Why?! Why?!", a small package arrived at the door from a dear friend. So I braved opening the parcel.

I was quite surprised to find a book by Graham Cooke. I often request his sermons when people ask what I want for Christmas gifts or birthdays, but my friend didn't know that. She left a bookmark in chapter four, which was titled: "The 'Why' Question Will Never Be Answered on Earth."[1]

I sat down and read the whole chapter. But maybe I just needed the title most. Maybe I needed to hear that *some* of my questions will never be answered this side of eternity. I needed to break the grip those whys had on me. I needed to surrender, one step closer to embracing all the unknowns.

Initially, giving myself permission to finally ask all my whys felt like breakthrough. But after a while, it didn't seem helpful to keep asking why in the long haul of loss. In fact, I could feel it sucking life out of me when I begged for a why to be answered. Especially, "Why me?" Because asking "Why me?" allows us to keep writhing in agony to the point we begin to feel like a victim.

Surrendering our whys can allow us to find answers to more satisfying questions. Even if we know the answer to our whys, it sadly won't change what happened. But if we start asking what or who or how, these questions seem to get us a lot further down the road toward healing.

Cooke offers alternative, more helpful questions that the disciples asked when Jesus ascended to heaven (found in Acts 2:17 and Acts 2:37): *What does this mean?* and *What shall we do?*[2]

We may not get an answer right away because some answers unfold with time. But we have nothing to lose if we start the asking. I've got nothing to lose, so I try to follow Cooke's advice.

Lord, I've lost Dan. What does this mean?

Then I remember and am comforted by God's words in Isaiah 54:5: *I am your Husband now.* Okay. Didn't expect an answer so soon. I want Dan back as my husband, but I receive Your invitation to take the load of weight and responsibility off my shoulders and transfer it to Yours. This means God will provide to pay my bills and help me raise my children. I guess I can handle that.

Lord, what am I supposed to do now? Like today.

When I ask this, the thought comes to me: "Eat breakfast." I smile. God knows I wanted to do something like save the world and change history. Somedays, He knows that I don't even want to move a muscle. God knows what I need most is simply to eat breakfast.

I used to have extensive daily to-do lists. But now, the Lord usually puts one thing on my mind for the day when I wake up. Somedays, I can do it. Somedays, that simple thing takes me a few days to finish. But this keeps my plate smaller when my world is caving in. I'm grateful that God only asks me to take one step at a time. One foot in front of the other.

There's one more question I learned to ask God that has been a personal favorite for decades:

Lord, who do "you want to be for me now, that you couldn't be at any other time?"[3]

To me, this question means what name or quality of God does He want me to come to know more intimately in *this* season. I brave asking Him and get quiet. *Defender.* Lord, I don't feel defended right now. *Trust me. Wait and see.* Well, okay. I'm all in.

It's good and well to ask all the questions: the hard ones, the good ones, and the ones that won't get us anywhere. But when we're ready to get some real answers or find some real peace, then let this be a gentle nudge to point you toward some fresh and new questions.

◆

Let's experiment to see if flipping your whys helps you make small steps forward.

Lord, I've lost my loved one, _____. What does this mean?

What am I supposed to do now? Like today?

And, Lord, who do You want to be for me right now? (Strong tower? Shield? Father? Brother? Comforter? Friend?)

This may be the best time of your life to experience God in a way you never have before. Write a prayer calling on that unique, particular name of God:

Thank You for leading me minute by minute,
hour by hour. You remember the frailty of my frame and
the weakness of my heart. Help me surrender my
whys to You. Help me rest knowing You can keep my
questions and their answers safe. Show me how
to move forward in love.

ISAIAH 54:5 • ACTS 2:37

Jesus asking why

Every moment that brought me to my knees, wailing, "Why? Why, God? Why?" brought me closer to the heart of Christ than maybe I was ready for. We pray to know His love and sometimes find ourselves carrying a cross in order to understand it. The very symbol of the Christian faith is a symbol of suffering and persecution, yet we lash out when suffering and persecution invade our stories. We want to taste His goodness, but we're surprised when the manna only falls in desert places. I never understood His sacrifice and bottomless love more acutely than in the moments when I shared in His suffering.

The day the whys flooded out on the bathroom floor was also the day I took up my own cross. Jesus didn't want His cross either. He questioned and asked if there was another way out. But when there wasn't, He surrendered it all.

What would happen if we give ourselves permission both to question and surrender, even if we don't get our answers?

Jesus surrendered all—calling out with a loud voice, "Father, into your hands I commit my spirit."[1] The Jews of Jesus' day had memorized the entire Tanakh, so they would've immediately recognized the words He spoke from Psalm 31, a prophecy of the cross that was fulfilled when He shouted those ancient words.

Jesus questioned why—saying in a loud voice, "My God, my

God! Why have you forsaken me?"[2] Hearing this, they would have recalled the entirety of Psalm 22, prophesying the mockery, physical agony, and piercing of His flesh. *Why have you forsaken me?*

However, we don't see Jesus getting a clear answer. At least not overtly. But Jesus lets us connect the dots—from the words He speaks on the cross back to Psalm 22 that foretold that day. And I think He did the same thing with the answer to why.

I believe that God, in all His intentionality, chose a man named Joseph to bury His Son. Maybe to remind us of Joseph's namesake, the man from the Old Testament,, the great-grandson of Abraham, grandson of Isaac, and favored son of Jacob. Seems like Joseph's story parallels much of Jesus' story. Both traded for money by "brothers," falsely accused, abused, abandoned, hated, taken for granted, and imprisoned unjustly. And God lifted both of them up to a place of honor at the right hand of a king. All their personal suffering redeemed for the sake of a bigger picture, the saving of many lives. Both could have judged their oppressors harshly, but they chose to show humility, forgiveness, compassion, and mercy instead.

Genesis 50:20 is where you'll find God's plan to redeem the evil plot of Joseph's brothers in order to save many nations through his devastating loss. Joseph's brothers, who left him for dead and then sold him into slavery, later found themselves at his mercy for their very lives. Joseph's response could've easily been vengeance. But mercy triumphs over judgment.[3] Essentially, Joseph replies, "Don't be angry with yourselves for selling me into slavery because God sent me here to preserve your life. It was for the deliverance of many."[4]

Joseph's response reminds me of Jesus saying, "Father, forgive them, for they know not what they are doing."[5] And Jesus knew the why—it was to rescue your very life and mine. It was for the deliverance of many. And He even endured the excruciating cross for the joy set before Him.[6]

During the season of Advent, we celebrate Jesus' coming to earth, and we wait for the day He comes back again. But aren't we surprised when part of His plan during our waiting season is for the kingdom to come to earth through our sharing in the cross?

During the first Christmas after my husband died, I sat down to read in the light of the Christmas tree. I started reading the introduction of *Chasing Vines* by Beth Moore until I was paralyzed by a flood of memories of Dan and me visiting the vineyards in Italy, California, even Nebraska—a vineyard with sweeping views so beautiful, we may as well have been in Tuscany. I finally broke down and let it all out as loudly as I could until it hurt my throat and my gut:

"Lord, where are Your angels? Where is Your Spirit? Where is Your presence? Where is Your defense? WHY HAVE YOU FORSAKEN ME?"

I didn't expect such a quick response, if any at all. In my spirit, it was so clear that it may as well have been audible. A paraphrase of Genesis 50:20. Why have you forsaken me?

For the deliverance of many.

As we continued that heated conversation in prayer, it brought me right back to where I started, bellowing, "BUT WHY HAVE YOU FORSAKEN ME?"

For the deliverance of many.

What if God really can use what was intended to harm me and flip it around to accomplish good, beautiful things? What if turning it around includes "the saving of many lives"?

Every time we cry out, "Why, God! Why have you abandoned me?" I guarantee it's because you've found yourself in that excruciating place of taking up your own cross. A time where you're being crucified with Christ and you no longer live, but Christ lives through you.[7] It's a time when you get to partake in His bitter sufferings. May you also know the sweetness of His joy, the saving joy set before Him. Could part of the answer to your "Why?" be "for the deliverance of many"?[8]

— ◆ —

If you've asked God your whys, did you get any inclinations or answers?

Can you relate to the stories of Jesus or Joseph in any way?

For some people, the promise of Romans 8:28 ruffles their feathers—that God can take what was intended to harm us and turn it for our good. How do you respond to that promise and why?

Have you felt forsaken by God? Write a prayer below and tell Him about it.

Father, thank You for being the kind of God
who takes what was meant for evil and turns it for our
good. And even more, for the deliverance of many.
Help me not disdain or discount that promise.
Help me not consider it trite, but to hold on to it
as truth. May this promise of good bring hope to my
heart again. In Jesus' name, amen.

PSALM 22 · PSALM 31 · LUKE 23 · GENESIS 50

blaming God for why

I put out "house fires" constantly. The washer self-combusted, and then the dryer died. The alternator is shot. Again. My eyes are bloodshot.

I offloaded some of my latest comedy of errors and plot twists to Samwise, a good listening friend. He looked at the gloomy sky and dark clouds blocking our view of the peaks today.

"I miss the mountains, Danita."

His words caused me to take a deep breath and remember the deepest ache in my heart, clouded by everything else that was—and still is—going wrong.

I miss my husband.

Samwise thumbed through the Word to get to Daniel. He read chapter three out loud, and it washed over me like hands and oil. God's Word just does that to me.

The quickest way to summarize Daniel 3 is grace under fire.

A Babylonian king threatens to throw Shadrach, Meshach, and Abednego into a blazing furnace if they refuse to worship said king. Instead, the three men remain devoted to the God of Abraham, Isaac, and Jacob. They reply to the king's threats, "If we are thrown into the blazing furnace, the God we serve is able to deliver us from it."[1] It took gutsy, bold faith to say that to the king. But they knew deep within them that God is mighty to save!

However, the best part is their next sentence: "But even if he does not," we will not worship your gods.[2] They knew God *could* save them from the blaze, but even if He didn't, they resolved within them to still praise God and only God. No matter the cost.

God, I know you can raise my husband from the dead, but even if You don't, I will still praise You. I know You can bring me justice after all that's been stolen, but even if You don't, I will praise You. God, I know You can get me out of this furnace, but even if You don't, I will still praise You. These words are hard to say, but they develop a fireproof faith inside of me.

How did the king respond? He was livid! He ordered to increase the furnace seven times hotter. It became so hot that the guards outside the furnace died.

The three men were firmly tied up and fell into the blaze. The men should've been burned to ash instantly like the guards, but onlookers watched them inside the fire unbound and walking around, alive! And they were not alone. There was a fourth man suddenly with them, and I think it was Jesus. The king was astonished. *How are they surviving this? And who is that other guy?* (You'll never believe what the king did next. Check out Daniel 3 to find out.)

I keep asking God, "When is this refining fire going to be good enough for You?" I felt like God kept turning up the heat, over and over. Like He was trying to get some gold buried way deep down. And I was fuming. But maybe that's not the right question after all.

As Samwise read this story over me, I was kind of beside myself. All this time, I've been blaming God for the natural consequences of our fallen world. God gave us freedom to make our own choices, and we often wield that freedom in less than loving ways (like that king and the guards and the authorities in my story and when I swear and call names). But God *always* uses His freedom to make sacrificial loving choices. Our decisions often lead us into being tied up, but God always offers a way out to be set free.

God didn't take away that king's freedom to make his own (poor) choices in order to prevent His people from such a trial. However, God chose to enter into that raging furnace *with* His people. Not only did Jesus save them, He also made sure they did not endure the blaze alone.

Do you ever wonder what it was like to see Jesus, whose eyes blaze with fire,[3] face-to-face? How did that moment mark those three men for the rest of their lives? Surely, they were never the same. Altered, refined, and made more beautiful.

When the men were set free, all the authorities crowded around in astonishment. How did the fire not scorch their clothes, singe their hair, harm their bodies? They didn't even smell like smoke. I bet Shadrach, Meshach, and Abednego were equally in awe that they were okay. I've had so many milestones and moments where I am in awe that I am okay. That I got out of bed that day and was able to walk around. Somehow, I knew that God was with me (even though He was painfully quiet), and I am not alone. This is grace under fire.

What's more, turning up the fire didn't harm them; it actually took out the enemy gatekeepers. The three men went in bound up and oppressed and came out of the fire unbound, set free, and with an intimate experience of the Emmanuel, the God with us. *Selah.*

God, we know You can save us,
but even if You don't,
we will praise You.

◆

Try to remember a moment or two where you were somehow able to do difficult things you never thought you'd have strength to do. (Getting through the funeral is definitely one of them.)

God, I know You can _____,
but even if You don't,
I will _____.

God, I know You can _____,
but even if You don't,
I will _____.

How has walking through this fire marked you? How do you want it to mark you?

Lord, I give You my heart. Make it burn in affection for Yours. Increase my trust in You. Forgive me for blaming You for things that You didn't do. Thank You for Your presence in these afflictions. Help me focus my thoughts more on You, the God who protects me and keeps me company in the fire, rather than on the one who is turning up the heat. In Jesus' name, amen.

DANIEL 3:8–30 • ISAIAH 43:2 • REVELATION 19:11–16 • HEBREWS 12:28–29

PART SIX

THE CROSSROADS

(faith + emotions)

the ministry of lament

In a culture that tries to stuff, distract, numb, and medicate, few people know about another healing alternative: lament. Lament is a healthy way to express the deep agony we experience in the tragedies we face. An honest heart cry, wail, or sob releases it. But lament takes it one step further and brings our grief before the Lord, asking Him to do something about it.

Some say that lament is a complaint or a whine. Others say it's something more refined. Bah. Let's not overcomplicate this.

A lament is simply getting honest with God about what's hard.

One of my favorite proverbs says that "an honest answer is like a kiss on the lips."[1] Being vulnerable and honest is refreshing and intimate. I'd much rather be in a heated, honest conversation than in a superficial one, pretending things are okay.

Before I discovered that proverb about honesty, I used to pretend with God. I never told Him how I really felt. I was afraid I'd hurt His feelings. And I wanted to protect Him from myself. I also was afraid to "go there" because I didn't know just how much junk might flood out once I got started.

With some experimenting, I've learned we *can* tell God everything in an honest way. Not only can God take it, but He actually welcomes and invites us to bring our hearts, worries, concerns, and hardships to Him. He gives us permission to feel what we need to feel. After all, He created these emotions and said that they are good.

I think a lot of Western believers get turned around in the intersection of faith and feelings. Like it's somehow not "holy" to feel deeply. Many other cultures are at home with big emotions, but Westerners are often scolded or judged for their emotions.

Feel it. Express it. It's okay. Jesus, Paul, Jonah, David, Joseph, Job . . . they all *deeply felt it*. And they didn't try to cover up and act like they didn't.

If honesty leads to intimate friendship, let's tell God how we feel. *Really* telling God how I felt abandoned by Him somehow brings me to this place of knowing He's right here. Been here all along.

Often, when I finally get the girls down for the night, the dishes and laundry done, lunches made, and the dog walked, I finally take time to lament and do some grief work. And that's healthy and mission critical, even if it costs me my normal early bedtime. It's only a season. But, my energy is scarce and my time is short. My lament usually ends up in tears, exhaustion, and, thankfully, a strange peace.

The majority of the time, lament ends in a resolved peace and trust. We end up deciding like Simon Peter, *If not You, God, then where else would I go?*[2] *I have no other viable options. No one else loves me like You do.* Other times lament brings us to our knees like Job, "Though he slay me, yet will I hope in him."[3]

While most lament does end in quiet resolution, my favorite psalms of lament don't. I appreciate the story of Jonah, where the prophet ends with, "It would be better for me to die than to live."[4] Jonah and David assure me that God never forces us to tie pretty bows around our deepest heartache.

The biggest victory in Jesus' ministry began with lament, so deeply troubled in His weeping that His sweat was like great drops of blood in the garden of Gethsemane.[5] When I map out the hugest breakthroughs in my life, all of them started with an honest lament too, pouring out to God where I'm really at and how bad things really are.

Writing your own lament is an ancient practice for good mental health, one our culture needs to re-remember. The fill-in-the-blank liturgy below is a simple way to get started. Feel free to whisper, declare, or cry it aloud.

A Liturgy for Lament

I feel forgotten and forsaken.

I feel weary and alone.

I feel betrayed and broken.

I feel _____ and _____.

I feel _____ and _____.

These are my honest feelings.

These are legitimate feelings.

My feelings are real, but they're not necessarily truth.

Here's what I know is true.

I am a child of God; His plans for me are good.

I am loved and _____ and _____.

I am accepted and _____ and _____.

When I cry out *Where are you?!,*

You whisper *here I AM.*

When my faith runs out,

You remain faithful to me.

I am a child of God; His plans for me are good.[6]

Father, please prepare my heart to be able
to be honest with You. Bring me to a time and a place
where I can tell You honestly how I really feel. I'm kind
of afraid of letting myself feel the intensity of this loss.
I'm nervous to tell You about how angry, devastated,
disappointed, disoriented, and lost I feel right now.
I may not be ready today, so prepare my heart to be
ready. Help me trust You with my emotions, no matter
how volatile they may be. In Jesus' name, amen.

PROVERBS 24:26 • JOHN 6:68–69 • JOB 13:15 • LUKE 22:44

when lament feels like puberty

I did a dumb thing. I looked in the mirror today. *Who is this haggard woman?*

I never knew that tears could actually turn white on your cheeks, like salt, like ash. My sister told me that different tears actually have different chemical properties. Tears from an onion are molecularly different from those of laughter or lament. (You can look it up for proof. I'm too tired.)

I've mourned before but never noticed ash manifest on my cheeks. The skin around my eyes is crêpe-y, and I hate these frowny lines between my eyebrows that won't go away.

As I try to mash that wrinkle flat with my thumb, I have deep thoughts. About puberty. I have tried and failed to block out seventh and eighth grade from my memory. I don't know a single person who says, "I'd love to relive junior high." The insecurity. The voice cracking. The new odors. The way you don't recognize yourself in the mirror. And everyone hits it differently, so you wonder if something's wrong with you because Stephanie got her B-cup and you're still in a trainer. *Training for what?*

Puberty is a turbulent, irrational season of life. You love and you hate within five seconds. It's a long season of lamenting the end of childhood and learning to rebuild and move forward as an adult-ish.

Sometimes, lament feels like reliving seventh grade. Some

lament is illogical. Some lament is accusatory. Most lament is absolutely and heartbreakingly justified. But the important piece is that we get honest with God about how we feel, even if what we feel isn't pretty or one hundred percent truth. In getting it out in the open, lament ushers in relief, and it gives us a starting place to meet the Lord. Lament opens the door to let the Comforter rush in.

> **Lament opens the door to let the Comforter rush in.**

Someone recently asked me, "What's troubling you?" A simple question that I felt fired up and ready to answer. I probably answered with a vague truthful statement like, "This is hard. It's harder than hard." But my full honest response overflowed onto the pages of my journal that night:

> *"What's troubling me today?"*
> You trouble me today, Lord.
> I'm struggling with I TRUSTED YOU to lead me, and
> now I just feel led on.
> And I'm struggling with how You think You're going to be
> glorified through this.
> And I'm struggling with . . .

My list went on for a while. (But I chose to spare you the details of my guts and lack of glory.) It wasn't pretty. But here's the deal. Lament may look ugly, but it opens the door to let the Comforter rush in. Grief often looks like a middle schooler's "I hate you!" and moments later, "Can you please rub my back?"

As soon as I was honest, it broke down all the pretenses between me and God. Honesty is the first step toward friendship. Even if it isn't "pretty" honesty. Even if my emotional honesty was not "biblical truth."

God is the safest place to bring our pain. Because He happens to be the only one who can enter in and heal. Jesus felt forsaken. It's okay if we feel that way too.

Think you can brave writing down what's troubling you today? What makes you feel angry or disappointed right now?

In the space below, scribble your pain back and forth. Get some of that frustration out. Use crayons or colors if you want. I choose red.

Lord, I'm struggling. Help me be brave and honest with
You, even if it doesn't look pretty. Help me take heart,
and help me take my heart to You. In Jesus' name, amen.

PSALM 42:3 • JOHN 16:33

the ministry of tears

Author Emily P. Freeman once explained that tears are messages from the truest beat of your heart that remind you where your heart beats most fully alive.[1]

Yes. My heart beats most fully alive with Dan. And so I welcome these tears.

What if tears are messengers?

Seldom do people check in. Often, it feels like nobody cares. But they did care. They cared so much that they wept for me and for Dan and for my girls. They wept so hard that they couldn't even pick up the phone. It changes my whole outlook. Their tears may have been the most powerful thing they could offer. This is the ministry of tears. These are times when the body of Christ is broken for you. The heart of Christ breaks for you. And not just in Jesus, but in Jesus-bearers, Christ-bearers, cross-bearers.

> **The heart of Christ breaks for you. And not just in Jesus, but in Jesus-bearers, Christ-bearers, cross-bearers.**

What if tears have a prayer language of their own?

When we think of the story of Lazarus, most people point out that Jesus wept. Seemingly surprised that Jesus cared that much. I think of it so differently. Of course He cared deeply. Nothing can separate us from Jesus' high and wide and never-ending boundless love. But what strikes me was the power in His tears.

What if tears are prayers?

Weeping comes from a depth that's gut-deep, bone-deep, soul-deep. And I believe when Jesus wept, it was also travailing prayer, stirring up a rebirthing power from the infinitely deep wells of His Spirit. After Jesus wept for Lazarus, life came from death. After Jesus wept in the garden, Life came from death. Search the Word and decide for yourself. But for me, that correlation is one I can't get over.

What if weeping is the birth pains of Resurrection power?

Jesus cried hard when He prayed. And often:

> During the days of Jesus' life on earth, he offered up prayers and petitions with fervent cries and tears to the one who could save him from death, and he was heard because of his reverent submission.[2]

The Holy Spirit also prays on your behalf with "groanings too deep for words."[3] What do you imagine that looks like? I picture weeping. Jesus is God with skin on, so if Jesus cries, God does too.

God cries *with* us and *for* us. He's not an indifferent, unfeeling God. The Scriptures are full of His passionate emotional responses to His children. So, if you have not been able to have your big cry, take comfort that He sees you and cries on your behalf.

Many feel a sense of shame, or they wonder what's wrong with them if they can't cry. I assure you that you're not the only one and that this doesn't mean anything is wrong with you. I imagine many things can keep back our tears, but the key is to remember that the body and mind have a way of pacing themselves.

Many say "there are no more tears in heaven," but the Bible doesn't actually say that. It says, "God will wipe away every tear from their eyes."[4] This means that there *are* tears in heaven and that God will brush them off our cheeks, one by one. I imagine, from what I know of Him, that He will take His time in doing so, mercifully, with loving kindness and tears streaming down His own glorious face as He wipes ours away.

In fact, the psalmist describes God collecting our tears in bottles in heaven.[5] Every tear you cried and every tear Jesus and others cried for you is seen, remembered, valued, and treasured. If He collects our tears, that means we never ever cry alone.

I suppose I record my tears in a book too when they fall onto the journal's page. The tears bleed the ink and serve as a landmark of sorts: "I cried here."

Sometimes, all we need is for someone to notice our tears. They don't need to say a word about it, but their soft eyes and gentle head nod says, "I see you. I acknowledge the heartache. I honor your tears."

When tears bleed the ink on the page, it also reminds me that my tears are both costly and powerful. I know God weeps for us. I've even had dreams of Dan weeping for us. The tears of a father are powerful, aren't they?

Why do you think God "bottles" our tears?

When did someone honor or acknowledge your tears? How did that make you feel?

Do you think tears carry power? Do you think tears can be unspoken prayers?

Do you hold tears back or embrace them? Do you react differently in different situations? Why do you think this is?

Healer, give me the ministry of tears. Release the tears that I've been holding back. I'm afraid they might consume me, Lord. So if I open these floodgates, please temper the rushing waters.

ROMANS 8:38–39 • REVELATION 21:4 • PSALM 56:8

when you want to give up

This morning, I told my friend Erika that I just want to give up. "What does that mean?" she asks, cautiously and wisely. "I don't know."

I don't really know what "I want to give up" means, but it's how I feel. I don't want to hurt myself. I just want to give up. It's hard to explain. *I think it means I don't want to take my life, but maybe it means I just feel dead inside already. And why get out of bed? And why go on? And why make dinner?*

Then I hear my daughter crying, reminding me of why. Life isn't only about me. And I die to myself all over again and check on her and figure out some cereal or something for dinner.

After tucking the girls in, I sit in our crickety rocker out back and look up at gray skies. All I can do is whisper, "Jesus. Jesus. Jesus." A flock of birds swoosh by like God whispering to my soul, "Child, I see you. It's going to get better. It's going to be worth it." The Holy Spirit beckons me once again to stay alive in the dead of winter.

"Oh, Lord. I trust you!"

I flashback to many seasons in my life when I wanted to give up. Depression and hopelessness, dark and heavy. I'd drive around in a fog and look up at the bleak winter sky, wondering why. And a whole flock of birds would swoop overhead, drawing my attention from the dark and heavy down below to the surprise of beauty and majesty above. Birds flew overhead often back then.

It's supernatural sometimes, when you feel like God's getting your attention, like with those flocks of birds. Especially if you're new to discovering God's voice and His active, attentive presence in your life. He truly draws near to the brokenhearted, but sometimes we don't know how to recognize Him. His communication is a love language all its own, because He knows you so intimately.

I kept wondering why the Holy Spirit seemed so active, revelatory, and chatty with me as I opened the Word before Dan died, and now . . . silence.

In loss or trauma, we can read the same sentence over and over and still not understand it. Even God's words on the page blur together and don't make sense.

Why, God? Why get quiet now when I need You most?

It took months of asking this question to see the answer. He got quiet because He knew all vocabulary, spoken or read, just blurred in the haze. But He didn't get silent as I had imagined. He just started communicating differently. He began speaking through birds overhead, airplanes over the mountains, and presence over words. He also started speaking through my journaling, dropping in revelation and guidance as I wrote. He started speaking through the mouths of my babies. He started speaking to me through worship songs like never before. And while I couldn't soak in hours of the Bible like before, I leaned into the stories I remembered.

When I want to give up, I remember Elijah who felt the same way. When starving and hunted down in the wilderness, Elijah cried out to God, "I've had enough!" While he was running for his life, he sat down, gave up, and asked God to end it. "Just let me die!" I don't think he really wanted to die. Maybe he just felt dead inside already.

How do you expect God might respond to a prayer like, "Just let me die!"? With a lecture or a scolding? Nope. The Father gave Elijah some angels, a nap, and some hot bread. And then another nap and more hot bread. It was enough to sustain him for the rest of his forty-day journey.[1]

When was the last time you had hot bread right out of the oven? With buuuuuutter. Remember the smell, the texture, how it made your eyes flutter closed and your belly comforted? Can you close your eyes a minute and go there?

God's Word is our hot bread. It's our daily bread.

If you find even one verse that connects with you, write it on a notecard or print copies and put them all over your house. Even one sentence of God's Word is hot bread that can sustain and nourish you for the long journey ahead. For me, I leaned on Psalm 31:7 and 1 Peter 5:10.

As I reread Elijah's story to share it with you, I had completely forgotten what comes next! And it's exactly what we've been talking about. When he gets to the mountain, he's looking and expectant for God's presence. But God doesn't come dramatically in the mighty wind, nor the earthquake, nor the fire. He comes in a way Elijah wasn't expecting Him. In a still, small voice.

Elijah teaches me a few things. I need to take more naps. (Or at least lay down and rest a bit.) I can be blatantly honest with God. Just a taste of God's Word comforts and sustains. And that God speaks in unexpected ways. Sometimes, we recognize God's presence even better in times of loss. Other times He feels very distant. That's when we remind our souls . . . just because He feels far, doesn't mean He is.

◆ ◆ ◆

What about you? Have you ever felt like you wanted to give up?

Have you struggled with thoughts of ending your life?

If so, the best thing you can do first is to tell somebody. A doctor, a pastor, a counselor, a friend. Do not fear calling for help. **Your life matters more than you know.** Encourage yourself that these thoughts will not last forever. Things will get better. **Your life matters more than you know.** If in immediate crisis, have courage and call 911. They will help you. Or you can call the Lifeline: 1-800-273-8255. They will help you. And pray this prayer as often as you need to:

> Lord, this is my SOS. Give me the courage to call for help and wisdom to know who to ask. You know everything I've been through. But You give me the power to overcome. Please help me find the medical, spiritual, and emotional support I need. Put the right people in my path. Protect my mind and heart from wanting to give up. I expose the lie that taking my own life would set me free. I declare that because Jesus Christ has set me free, I am free indeed (John 8:36). I align myself with the truth, that true freedom is found in Jesus. I declare that my vindication is from the Lord. Fill me with peace and joy as I trust in You (Romans 15:13). The future feels bleak and hopeless right now, but give me courage to believe that Your goodness and mercy will follow me all the days of my life (Psalm 23:6). Help me trust You more and give me hope for my future. Strengthen my inner being to come to know and believe the unshakable, unconditional love You have for me (1 John 4:15–16).

— ◆ —

Today, does God feel close or far?

Do you ever notice little ways God might be trying to get your attention?

When did you feel like God sent angels or people to care for your physical or emotional needs when you wanted to give up? If you've got nothing, write a prayer asking for that.

Find one verse that comforts, encourages, or sustains you. Write it on a notecard and stick it by your mirror.

Father God, when I feel dead inside, raise me
back to life. When I feel numb and hopeless, resurrect
my hope. When I want to give up, give me rest and
nourishment for both my body and my soul. Give me
ears to hear Your still small voice. Give me eyes to
recognize Your presence. Lord, have You been trying
to connect with me in a new way? Show me the ways
You're trying to get my attention.

1 KINGS 19

the ministry of smoke alarms

Author Lysa TerKeurst says it this way, "Feelings should be indicators, not dictators."[1]

Our emotions are quite helpful and gracious if we listen to them and allow them to have their own voice. Emotions can alert us that there's a problem, but they do not get to rule and reign over our behavior. Outbursts are like the indicator light on the car's dashboard. This alerts us at the beginning of a problem and allows us to get it serviced or fixed before it becomes a very dangerous problem.

Sometimes we're afraid of our emotions. We may even feel bullied, controlled, or victimized by our emotions if we don't understand this principle. But if we listen to what our emotions are saying, we can get the help we need before a potential problem gets out of control. When we think of our emotions as indicators, it helps us know when we need to engage in better self-care or soul-care. For instance, if we're feeling extra weepy or angry or volatile, this is our body's way of telling us that we may need more rest or we may need to pray for peace. When I notice I'm losing my cool, that's an indicator to me that I need to put myself in time-out. Grown-up time-outs look like a nap on the hammock, a cup of tea, or a walk outside.

I know a lot of people who say they're not emotional, but that they do get angry. I'm always baffled by this logic. Um. Anger *is* an emotion. And it's a perfectly fine emotion to feel. I learned this from watching my friend Erika as she instructed and steadied her three-year-old son. He wanted to lash out, but she remained calm: *It's okay to feel angry, but it's not okay to hurt yourself or other people because of your anger.*

This is a revolutionary distinction. Most of us are raised to think that anger is inherently bad. Anger is not bad; it's often helpful. Anger is like a smoke detector going off. It's loud, alarming, and can make you feel afraid, but that smoke detector is telling you that something is *not* right so you can do something about it.

Righteous anger is a thing. Don't you get mad when one of your kids hits their sibling? Don't you feel mad when someone steals from you? Don't you get mad when someone is harmed or harms themselves or suffers an illness or accident?

God is passionate and fiercely protective. He loves justice and hates what's evil. Trust me, God feels angry too. Have you ever read Isaiah? God gets angry when His kids let evil and darkness rule their hearts. Because He knows how destructive that is to us and those around us. I bet you He often feels angry right alongside you.

What's not okay is when we direct that anger toward someone else in violent actions or words. God's Word tells us to uproot anger for the sake of being angry because it only cultivates evil.[2] It's not okay when we direct that anger inward toward ourselves in any forms of self-punishment or self-destructive behavior. Yes, alcoholism, cutting, or drug addiction. But also "overdosing" on Netflix, work, or ice cream.

Just because we're grieving doesn't mean we can treat ourselves or others harshly. In our lowest and most broken places, we often need to apologize, not for feeling angry, but for how we hurt others out of our anger. The good news is that asking for forgiveness is the first step to being set free.

———— ◆ ◆ ◆ ————

Let's let our smoke alarms indicate where we need to take better care of ourselves. Notice any smoke alarms going off in you lately? What conversations, memories, or situations usually trigger your anger? Ask God for healing in those areas.

How do you usually express your anger?

Can you think of a better way to express and direct your anger next time? Brainstorm restorative ways you can put yourself in grown-up time-out when the alarms go off:

Do you need to apologize to someone because of how you might have hurt them?

Are you angry with yourself about anything? What do you need to forgive yourself for? Ask God to forgive you too and then use your red pen and cover anything you've written with "forgiven."

Prince of Peace, when You created me, You put these emotions in me. They're God-given gifts. Help me embrace, feel, and express them. Help me be honest with You. I'm grateful Your response is never condemnation but always unconditional love for me. Even when I'm feeling rotten. Forgive me for the ways I've turned on You, myself, and others in my anger. Help me be courageous enough to say I'm sorry. Help me forgive myself too. In Jesus's name, amen.

PSALM 37:8 • PROVERBS 15:1, 18

PART SEVEN

THE VEIL BETWEEN HEAVEN AND EARTH

(you + your loved one)

the what ifs

When Dan prepared for deployment years ago, my mind was full of one phrase: "What if . . .?" I looked up into the humid Florida sky past those palm trees and begged God to keep my husband safe. That evening, when each of these questions rose up in my heart one by one, I saw assurance in the heavenlies, like a celestial call and response.

"What if he doesn't come back?"
Shooting star!
"What if the worst happens?"
Shooting star!
"What if that's the last time I ever hold him again?"
Shooting star!

The shooting stars didn't answer my questions, but they told me He heard my cries. That night, I resolved to trust God regardless. Sometimes when we want answers, God gives us signs and wonders instead. God responded to my doubtful *what ifs* by turning my question around:

"What if God is able?"
"What if He is who He says He is?"
"What if He is trustworthy?"

I found that these transformed *what ifs* led me to a place of peace, trust, and hope for my future. Whereas, my previous *what ifs* only gave fear permission to lead me by the collar.

In that deployment season, I quickly and dramatically changed how I asked my questions. I still asked plenty of questions. Asking God questions is needed and healthy. But I think the things we ask and the way we ask them can either help us or hinder us.

However, in loss, the *what ifs* are a whole different beast. In addition to worry about the future, they're also filled with the regrets of the past. The enemy tries to make us feel like the loss was our fault. Like somehow, we could've played God and spared our loved one's life.

"What if I just put my foot down and told him not to go? Maybe he'd still be here."

"What if we didn't go out that night? Then this never would have happened."

"What if I took different supplements? Maybe I could've saved the baby?"

On top of that, grief has *what ifs* of an anxious future as well.

"What if we never get pregnant again?"

"What if I can't pay my bills?"

"What if I end up alone for the rest of my life?"

Whenever the *what ifs* come to you, record them below. When you bring the judgmental voice of the enemy out from the darkness and into the light, it loses power.[1] Journaling or talking about it exposes the voice of the accuser and his lies.

Losing Dan slowly highlighted numerous regrets, ways I wish

I loved and respected him better. Even in the healthiest relationships, we remember ways we hurt the one we love. When memories resurface of how I failed him or hurt him, I whisper, "I'm so sorry, Dan," or "I wish I could have loved you better." I don't know if he can hear me, but it's good for my heart to apologize. I tell God I'm sorry too.

A treasured friend of mine, Quin Sherrer, author of *Hope for a Widow's Heart*, explains how a widow named Marie settled on a beautiful way to handle this. When she wants to share something with her late husband, she simply talks to God about it and asks God to relay the message for her.[2] This feels good to me. Sometimes, I ask God to tell Dan that I'm sorry or I love him and miss him or thank you.

But there's so much we wish we could still say to our loved ones once they're gone, isn't there? Healing and resolution can also be found in writing a letter to your loved one. Especially helpful if you didn't get to say goodbye, if there's complex grief, or if it was a wounding relationship. Tell them in the letter what hurts, what was unjust, and also offer forgiveness. Then lay your letter to rest in the care of Jesus.

When regrets surface, it's important to discern where these regrets originate. Our soul trying to learn from our past? The Holy Spirit inviting us into forgiveness and healing? Or the accuser trying to heap guilt on us?

The enemy roams the earth looking for someone to devour and destroy.[3] But God roams the earth looking to strengthen and encourage us.[4] Since they're polar opposite, you'd think it'd be easy to figure out where our thoughts are coming from. But the deceiver is pretty good at deceiving. So here's how I discern the difference.

When a memory returns to my mind full of condemnation and

shame, telling me it's my fault or telling me how stupid that was, it's the enemy. His goal in resurfacing memories is to steal your joy, kill your hope, and destroy your peace.[5] He enjoys oppressing us by replaying our wrongdoings or even making up make-believe wrong doings. While the enemy isn't all-knowing, he definitely is the father of lies. Darkness wants us to agree with the false whispers. You can take authority over these type of thoughts by saying, "No. I will not receive condemnation or shame in Jesus' name." What's more, if you turn the regret or worries into a prayer, then the peace of God will watch over you.[6]

When a memory comes with gentleness, and sometimes remorse, and a desire to usher peace and healing, it's the Lord. Jesus is gentle and lowly at heart.[7] He understands our temptations and sufferings.[8] He came to lift the heaviness off of you and heal you. Jesus' goal is to renew your joy, overflow your hope, and increase your peace. He came to bring you freedom and life. Jesus never ever condemns you.[9]

So, pay attention to the motive and the tone of these regrets and what ifs as they surface. There's a distinct difference between grace and condemnation, and I invite you to pay attention.

Have courage. Try to write out your honest worrisome, doubtful, fearful, or regretful *what ifs*.

- What if . . .
- What if . . .
- And what if . . .

Be braver still and talk to God about your *what ifs*, your worries, and your regrets. He really can handle hard questions. Hang there a minute and listen. How does He respond?

Now let's ask God to help you reframe your *what ifs*. Write a new list of *what ifs* that go from fear-based questions to faith-based questions. Think of these as declarations in question form.

- "What if God really is near to the brokenhearted?"
- "What if God really is the Father to the Fatherless?"
- "What if He really is the Defender of the Widow?"

- What if . . .
- What if . . .
- What if . . .

Here's a simple prayer you can pray out loud whenever a regret or condemning memory resurfaces:

A Liturgy for Regret
To the memories of how I messed up,
Grace is enough.
To the memories that haunt me,
Grace is enough.
To the memories that shame me,
Grace is enough.

Redeemer, what if You are who You say You are?
Renew my mind and heart. Deliverer, lift off guilt,
condemnation, self-condemnation, and shame from me.
Heal the regrets and haunting memories that resurface.
Savior, forgive me. And help me forgive myself.
I wish I could have loved him better. You're the only one
who can deliver me and set me free.

ROMANS 8:1 • JOHN 10:10 • 2 CORINTHIANS 12:9
2 CORINTHIANS 10:3–6

the coulda-woulda-shouldas

Years after the "what if" shooting stars, I found myself at the trailhead where Dan went missing. I stared up the shadowed cliffs and pines that night. I rotated between crying, singing worship songs, and saying prayers. I finally looked upward to the night sky, with a sacrifice of praise, whispering, "Lord, I lift Your name on high."

Shooting star.

Later my mind raced with what we should have done or could have done differently. But then I remembered something Dan taught me, and so I repeated the phrase out loud, "No coulda-woulda-shouldas."

Shooting star.

I remembered when Dan and I saw a shooting star the night he proposed. Sometimes when we want answers, God gives us wonders instead.

Those two phrases, divinely punctuated by shooting stars, carried me through the days and months ahead. Literally like guiding lights. Holy, divinely placed punctuation marks in the sky.

"Lord, I lift Your name on high."

In some strange economy of mercy, praising God keeps us from crumbling. He is strong, able, and trustworthy. And when we tell Him so, He calms the

> Sometimes when we want answers, God gives us wonders instead.

storm, silences our fears, and hides us under His wing. Whenever we think about whatever is good and true and beautiful, the peace of God floods our hearts. Well, He is the most good, most true, and most beautiful thing you will ever lay eyes on. If you keep your heart and mind focused on the Lord and His goodness and mercy, you will have perfect peace.[1] Perfectly unexplainable, undeniable peace. Just so, we sing an ancient psalm: "I lift my eyes up to the mountains—where does my help come from? My help comes from the LORD, the Maker of heaven and earth."[2]

"No coulda-woulda-shouldas."

When the accuser comes around and tries to slip in condemnation, that phrase shuts him up. "No coulda done this better. No woulda done that differently. No shoulda said this instead."

The heart wants to go back and redo things. The mind wants to rewrite the story so that we can save the day in our imaginary hindsight. But this only leaves us defeated, not victorious. And the accuser jumps on that opportunity to hit you while you're down. Control sneaks in to tell you that you could have changed the outcome. But that's not fair to the heart and those voices do not speak out of Love. Quickly silencing "coulda-woulda-shouldas" brings me back to the place of abiding trust and peace. Wishing this or that was handled otherwise isn't going to change the situation. Just so, we sing:

> All to Jesus, I surrender,
> All to Him I freely give;
> I will ever love and trust Him,
> in His presence daily live.
> I surrender all. I surrender all.
> All to Thee, my blessed Savior,
> I surrender all.[3]

What's beautiful about God is He practices what He preaches. In fact, Jesus was the originator of that phrase![4] We sing to Him, but He first sings over us.[5] The Holy Spirit is with you, singing over you today whether your ears are tuned to hear Him or not. He guides your steps as beautifully as He orders the North star that shines constant and the shooting stars that only last a breath but take your breath away.[6]

Like your beloved. And mine.

Try to recall a time when you received a sign, a provision, or a wonder:

Things I wish I coulda-woulda-shoulda done differently:

Now, grab that red pen and write over your coulda-woulda-shoulda list above. You can write "forgiven," "grace," "canceled," "freedom," or whatever feels most healing. It's just a tangible way to see your regrets hidden under the mercy of God. As you do, declare, "I cover over all of this in the blood of Jesus."

Keeper of the stars, open my eyes to see
Your signs and wonders. Help me lean on You
and not my own understanding.[7] I've blamed myself,
others and You. Help me believe it's not my fault. Help
me surrender these unanswerable questions. Give
me resolve and strength to not give in to any coulda-
woulda-shouldas. Increase my trust in You.

ISAIAH 26:3 • PHILIPPIANS 4 • ROMANS 15:13 • PSALM 19:1–4

the could-be, would-be, should-bes

I lift my eyes to the mountains and blinding sun, marveling at how the clouds glow over the peaks. Reminds me of the men who talked with God on top of the mountains . . . Moses, Enoch, and my Beloved. I'm amazed the sting isn't here today even though it's the second wedding anniversary I've survived without my husband. I feel refreshed after an actual night of sleep. That's God moving mountains right there. I feel hopeful, and the mountains look heavenly.

But when I turn away and look down, I see snow drifts billowing up to our front door. This is the biggest blizzard Colorado's had in years. Mountains of overwhelm drift in. I begin to buckle. I can't do this. Shoveling isn't what I should be doing today.

Today we *should* be celebrating thirteen years of marriage *together*. I *should* be putting my hair in rollers and picking out a dress to go dancing in. Dan *would* be outside right now digging us out from under the tundra. The girls *would* be playing with him, building the most epic snow igloo. He made snow fun.

Why does our house seem perfectly positioned to catch all the neighborhood's snow? Why can't I even open our front door because the snow is piled so high over here but the neighbor's dusting of snow is already melting in the sun? Why am I taking this personally today, feeling so burned and buried?

It's often and rightly said, "Comparison is the thief of joy." I rarely fall for that trick, but today looks like I let the thief come right in and take it.

It's tricky. There's nothing wrong with our "could-be, would-be, should-bes." They are the mind's way of sorting what was once and what is now. And it's important to acknowledge them. I'm sure you've felt the tension where your old reality clashes with your new one. Sometimes could-be, would-be, should-bes arrive as sorrowful remembrances, but other times they swell into rage, resentment, or comparison.

This morning, I had joy and peace when I focused on where my help and rescue came from. But soon as I started looking around, I melted down. That is the power of worship and praise: that you become who you gaze upon. Looking at other families and happy couples, I become a frail frame of a chronically-ill widow. But gazing upward toward my God, peace washes over so gently I almost don't notice it. And the joy that strengthens my bones rises up so organically, I almost overlook its presence. But it's there. And I notice the difference strikingly as soon as I begin to face the other way.

Milestones are particularly painful because those days mark well what would, could, or should be and the people we love who are no longer present. The child who would be three years old today. The couple who would be celebrating their 50th today. The mom who could be here to help with that big decision today. The grandpa who could be playing with the kids today.

For military families, deployment timeframes add another trigger for what *should* be. My little one and I often confide in each other, "I don't feel like Daddy is really gone. I feel like he's just deployed." At seven and a half months out, our body and minds remember, assuring us, "He should be home any day now." During the seventh, ninth, and tenth month after Dan's death, I often pulled back the curtains at the front door, looking for his return. The months thereafter got increasingly harder. If that's you and your children today, I want you to know you're not alone.

The snowdrifts out my window are too much. I listen to my body and firmly decide I cannot shovel this today. If it doesn't break my back, it may break my heart.

A few hours later, I see kind neighbors outside my window, shoveling me out once again like snow angels. Thankfulness overwhelms me. God shows up for me in my weakness and despair and digs me out all over again. Today was a hard one, but we weathered the storm once again.

This is where gratitude sneaks into the enemy's camp and steals my joy back for me again.

What would you be doing, could you be doing, or should you be doing with your beloved today?

Have any recent or upcoming milestones heightened your awareness of your would-be, could-be, should-bes?

What do you make of the could-be, would-be, should-bes? What shall we do with them?

Do you notice comparison stealing your joy? How can you actively get it back today?

Lord, help me keep my thoughts on Your goodness and Your mercy instead of the overwhelm in front of me. Help me notice when comparison and self-pity try to sneak in. Help me guard my joy with gratitude. Show me how to gently handle my could-be, would-be, should-bes as they come up. Help me accept that this is my lot. You are my Rescuer; You are where my help comes from.

PSALM 40:2 • PHILIPPIANS 4:11–13 • MATTHEW 28:2–6 • PSALM 121 *the veil between heaven and earth*

When you sit on the front row at a funeral, you find your-self in the place where the veil between heaven and earth grows strangely thin. I felt like I was operating in two realms simultaneously, with one foot in the natural and another in the spiritual. And it felt like Dan was there with us. No, I don't believe in ghosts, and I'm not much into sci-fi. But everyone I know who has lost a loved one mentions this phenomenon. Leaves me wondering how heaven works.

Before my husband died, he signed me up to attend a writing conference later that fall. I decided to go to the conference in honor of Dan and his support for my writing. One evening, the organizers lit a huge bonfire at the barn with food trucks and blankets and pillows everywhere. As I walked through the field filled with parked cars, I looked out at the scene. The buzz of excitement, all the people, the flickering flames and clouds above. I noticed a license plate from Georgia with a bumper sticker about running. It reminded me of Bethany, one of my fellow writing friends from Georgia who passed away just as suddenly as Dan. None of it makes earthly sense.

I couldn't help but think of Dan sending me here and how much I wished Bethany could be here too. I looked back up at the bonfire and suddenly, the veil between heaven and earth grew thin again. I don't know how heaven works, but it felt like Dan and Bethany were both very near, right there above the crackles of the fire, cheering me on and celebrating this gathering of beautiful people.

Our loved ones seem to have a special ministry to us in ways we can't always explain. In ways the Bible doesn't explain either, leaving it to mystery. But these are places where heaven feels very close to earth.

My friend and author Kim Erickson told me about when her three-year-old son died from strep. As he was fading from earth (or rather, as he was coming to life in Christ), he said to her, "Oh, Mommy! It's so beautiful here." After he died, she learned all she could about heaven and the Bible, and then gave her life to Jesus. She gave her life's work to Jesus too, and wrote *Surviving Sorrow* which has brought healing to so many.

And then there is the ministry of dreams. After my friend Samantha lost her husband, he came to her in dreams. He told her heaven is real. *Go toward the light. Read the Bible. Teach our children. Go to church. Learn about it. Heaven is real!* When she woke up, she opened her Bible for the first time in almost ten years! She became a Jesus follower, was baptized in the ocean, and is falling in love with a God who cherishes her. A God she never knew before her late husband told her about Jesus in dreams.

It's only natural to imagine where our person is and what they're doing. I've personally decided my husband is still working and encouraging in heaven. Can't prove it, but if there was work in the garden *before* the fall, then work is very good. It's a beautiful thing to God, to both rest and to work. I imagine Dan prays in heaven too. If Jesus and the Holy Spirit pray in heaven, wouldn't the saints follow His example? The Scriptures give us hints of heaven, but leave much to mystery. All I know for sure is my husband is alive. He's more fully alive in Christ now than he's ever been before.

But I've lost many loved ones who didn't lead lives of faith. It's natural to feel concerned about where they are now. When I do, the Holy Spirit always reminds me of the thieves on the cross. Both led profoundly criminal lives. One mocked Jesus to his death. But the other called out to Jesus with his last breath. With a simple prayer, he said to Jesus, "Remember me when you come into your kingdom." Jesus assured the man, "Today, you'll be with me in paradise."[1] The man on the cross gives me great hope. I've heard several stories of people who almost died and gave their lives to Christ in their last breath. I take great comfort in that.

Our residence in heaven or hell is not based on how we lived our lives. It's based on our faith in Christ. (Religiosity will not like the sound of that, but it's the Good News!) We may not get to know the last intimate conversation a person has with their Maker, but we can entrust their life, death, and salvation to the God of mercy who gave up everything to save them. We can rest assured that all who call on the name of the Lord shall be saved.[2]

When we have to make decisions or problems arise, it's also only natural to wish we could ask our deceased loved one for advice or direction. But God's Word warns us not to: "When someone tells you to consult mediums and spiritists, who whisper and mutter, should not a people inquire of their God? Why consult the dead on behalf of the living?"[3] If you've done this, confess it and ask God to forgive you. With authority in Jesus Christ, close all the spiritual doors you have opened between darkness and yourself, your family, and generations after you. Cover it all in the powerful blood of Jesus Christ that washes away every sin and cleanses us from all darkness. Instead, when you want to seek counsel or guidance, consult the Wonderful Counselor, the compassionate God who sees the beginning and the end, the Author of your faith.

Scriptures tell us plenty about how heaven and earth operate, but they also leave much to mystery. When we find ourselves where the veil between heaven and earth grows thin, may it increase our sense of wonder and awe in the God "who is able to do immeasurably more than all we ask or imagine."[4]

What questions do you have about how heaven and earth operate?

Have you experienced a time where the memory of your beloved was so strong, they almost felt present? A dream, a vision, a sign. Write it down so you don't forget.

What do you think of this phenomenon? Think I'm crazy? Or can you relate?

Lord, there's so much I don't understand
about how heaven and earth work. But I do know
that I feel stretched thin between the two. And it's painful.
Strengthen me to know how much You love me.
And minister to me by bringing me good memories of
my beloved. I confess putting You in a box of what
I think You can or can't do. Give me ears to hear and
eyes to see Your work in my life. Help me study Your
Word and show me great and mysterious things
I do not know.[5] In Jesus' name, amen.

HEBREWS 12:1–3 • JEREMIAH 33:3 • 2 CORINTHIANS 5:1–10

the legacy of prayer

My preschooler said to me, "Mommy, did you know there's someone in heaven who loves God and still teaches people to love each other?"

I asked, "Is it Daddy?"

"No."

"Grandpa Lowell?"

"No."

"He teaches us to love each other from heaven no matter if our skin is brown or pink."

"Ohhh. Martin Luther King Jr.?"

"Yes!"

Martin Luther King Jr. still teaches people to love each other. He sure does. His life and legacy remain actively teaching us to this day to love one another. And his dreams are still coming true.

Months after this conversation, I woke up from a dream about MLK with a strong revelation: "The dream doesn't die with the dreamer." Somebody needs to hear that today. *Dreams don't die with the dreamer ... and neither do their prayers.*

If you're like MLK, like our faithful prayer mentors, or like my husband Dan, then you pray that your God-given dreams will come to fruition. We dream of heaven on earth, and therefore, we pray His kingdom will come. Martin Luther King Jr. and countless others have laid up prayers for reconciliation and freedom that are still being answered to this day. His prayers did not stop working when he died. And neither did Dan's. This is the legacy of prayer. I take comfort that the prayers Dan laid up for our family and the prayers MLK laid up for our nation are *still* powerful and effective and ever reaching.[1] When we pray for the generations that come after us, those prayers reach out ahead of us like dreams. We sow prayers and trust that "the seed of the righteous shall be delivered."[2] Prayer is scattering seed into the future, spiritual deposits in generations who've not even walked the earth yet.

When I discussed the legacy of prayer with a fellow companion in sorrow, she sent me this quote. Mark Batterson explains it perfectly:

> God will answer our prayers in the lives of [both natural and spiritual] offspring we won't meet until the Father's family reunion at the marriage supper of the Lamb. But every prayer we pray, every gift we give, every sacrifice we make, every step of faith we take is an inheritance left to the next generation. And our prayers live on, long after we die, in their lives.[3]

Doesn't that make you want to pray more? Not only do our prayers mysteriously actually work, but they also work for generations beyond us!

During the days when Dan was missing, many people had dreams and visions that he was alive. Because of those dreams, we fought for it boldly in prayer. When my prayer team and I prayed for Dan to be raised from the dead, God brought a picture to mind of sunflowers growing up out of his feet. I thought for sure that meant God would bring him back to life.

But those dreams didn't come true the way we expected. Those prayers weren't answered as we'd hoped. Later, the casket was closed for the last time, and we drove to the burial site. On our way, I saw hundreds of sunflowers rising up out of concrete along the highway. On that long, somber drive, I wrote this:

There's no abundant harvest
Without seed, broken and buried.

Seeds are tiny caskets, buried in holes in the ground. Seeds are dreams, crushed and broken. Seeds go quiet and unseen for a time and then rise up out of the dark, cold earth with new life. In Nebraska, we buried seeds in the earth and stuff actually grew! We marveled as little shoots grew as tall as us, full of poblanos and Brussels sprouts. How does this happen? How can you bury hope in seeming nothingness and then beauty and fruit come up? Seeds are as mysterious as prayer.

And dreams are the seed of the righteous. My old pastor taught me that sometimes the one who is given a dream is not the one who sees the dream to fulfillment. For example, King David was passionate about his God-given vision to build the temple, but he never saw it to fruition. His vision was fulfilled by his son, King Solomon. Sometimes we sow God's dreams, and other times we fulfill the God-given dreams of those before us.

Our children are also the seed, dreams and answered prayers of the righteous. MLK planted dreams and seeds that are still being raised up today. The truths we plant in our children and the prayers we pray for our children will continue on. And the dreams our loved ones leave in us don't have to die with our dreamer. They can still come true.

An old friend from Nebraska, who knew nothing about my sunflower stories, sent me a vase of sunflowers. On the card, she wrote:

"Like a sunflower, may you and your children keep following the Son and growing and blooming in the Valley."

As I typed up those words, my oldest came into the office holding a sunflower shoot in a paper cup! My youngest had grown that sunflower at school as a Mother's Day gift. (My children are also my dreams come true.) And without knowing the timeliness of her words, my youngest was in the other room, singing her own made-up song, "Heaven's dreams come true! Heaven comes to earth!" Can we just let that all sink in?

Surely, dreams don't die with the dreamer, and answers to our prayers outlive us. May heaven's dreams come true in your heart and home, on earth as it is in heaven.

What or who are your God-given dreams that have come true?

What big dreams did you have with or for your loved one?

Can you entrust those dreams to the Lord for safekeeping? Write a prayer doing so:

Did your loved one have dreams for you that you need to hold on to or let go of?

Father, I feel crushed when I think of the dreams
we had for our future. I entrust my dreams to You for
safekeeping. Give me the grace and trust I need to
release these dreams into Your hands. And help me leave
my own legacy of prayer. Raise our God-given dreams
back to life. Restore our hope, God, and let us
be like those who dream dreams.

PSALM 145:1–13 • PSALM 126:1 • ACTS 2:17–21 • HOSEA 10:12

PART EIGHT

SACRED GROUND

(hope of redemption)

when it hits the fan

Did I mention I picked up swearing? I'm trying to quit. For a solid month (or three, it's all a blur), the "s-word" was a favorite. Needing better vocabulary, I asked around for suggestions. I sought wisdom from my mom, my best friend, and a few others. I decided that maybe I should start running instead of swearing? That lasted about five feet.

In desperate moments, when I'm at my wits' end, I cry out, "Lord, I just want fruit! If I have to live through this hellish time, I want to see the fruit of it." Essentially, I'm saying, "Oh God, make this worth it!" I'm saying, come through big for me because right now, I'm knee-deep in manure.

Ironically, cow manure is exactly what is needed to grow and produce fruit. And if you want green grass, chicken scat will be your best friend. Gardeners and farmers actually pay good money for this. We actually *need* fertilizer to nourish the earth. *This* makes for the richest soil and best conditions for crops to fruit and grow.

We talked about how Joseph got dealt more "fertilizer" than anyone else I can recall in the Bible. (Save Jesus.) But he also saw more fruit in his lifetime than I can imagine!

So now when I'm tempted to swear, I stopped using the "s-word" and switched to the "f-word." *Fertilizer!*

By naming the tough stuff I'm enduring "fertilizer," it reminds me that there are redeeming qualities to this foul smelling and offensive substance. There's redemption to be had!

Fertilizer makes for fertile soil; fertile soil makes for a rich, abundant harvest of fruit.

While I will not arrogantly declare, "Bring it on!", I can at least have that unspoken confidence—the solid trust that God will till this fertilizer into the soil and turn it out for my good and for the deliverance of many.

"You intended to harm me, but God intended it for good to accomplish what is now being done, the saving of many lives."[1]

Because my Redeemer *always* gets the final say.

Aftertaste

Father,
we need to talk.
Today, I did not turn the other cheek.
But today, I was a persistent widow
Today, I fought for what's right
(or was it my pride?)

Father,
we need to talk.
Today I did not choose to speak life.
I did not become more like Christ.
But today, I said I'm sorry.
And I am.

Father,
we need to talk.
When they spit in my face
I didn't ask You to step in.
I just said bleepity bleep bleep—
ugly words on pretty little lips.

Father,
we need to talk.
But could You first wash
my mouth out with soap?

Wanna get a little messy? Let's call out all the fertilizer in your life by name. List all the fertilizer in your life:

Now put your hands on the page over your list of fertilizer and pray, "God, redeem all of this. Turn this for good."

Now grab your trusty red pen and ask God for holy imagination. Try to write over your fertilizer ways you could see glimmers of redemption in these things. And if you've got nothing, just cover it all in "the blood of Jesus."

Father, the compounded stress got to me.
Forgive me for my mouth. Let no unwholesome speech
come out of my mouth.[2] Help me speak life and
not death over people around me.[3] Help me trust that
You care about the "fertilizer," and You hate the stench
as much as I do. Help me trust that if I have to
walk through this, You will work it together for my good
and for the deliverance of many.[4] Thank You
that tomorrow morning, your mercies are new![5]
Fresh start with a clean mouth. In Jesus' name, amen.

JOHN 5:17 • GENESIS 50:20 • 2 CORINTHIANS 4:17–18 • ROMANS 8:18

when the Holy Spirit takes the wheel

Yesterday, I folded laundry and tried talking myself out of packing. The girls asked with hope and joy, "Are we going back to visit Nebraska?!" *No.* Within two hours, all our bags were packed. If you know how I normally pack with meticulous lists, this is nothing short of miraculous.

"Are we going?!" *Only if I sleep tonight.*

The next morning, "Are we going!?" *No. Mommy didn't sleep at all.*

Remember how I said driving is hard for me? I wasn't going to brave this road trip. So, how am I here? Driving down one-lane, back-country Kansas? In the dead of winter? I can't believe I'm doing this. Should I turn back? But I know the presence of God will be there, and I am desperate for His presence.

We arrive into the fold of old friends who hold us and weep with us. How we've needed them. (The driving pulled two ribs out of place, made breathing painful, and cost me three chiropractic adjustments. But it was worth every painful breath!)

One of Dan's best buddies Eric-san and his wife Sarita greet us and graciously give up their room for us to sleep in. On their dresser, I notice a statue of a couple holding each other. The sign beside it speaks of marriage and being best friends forever. We used to go out dancing on double dates with this couple. Flashbacks of sambas, tangos, and laughter weigh in like great pain. I long for Dan.

Longing. Here's where English falls short sometimes. My Brazilian friends have a word that English doesn't have: *saudade*. They taught me that saudade is an intense longing, a soulful painful nostalgic missing of someone you love. I never compared *saudade* to sorrow before. But I think they're cousins. After a good hot shower, I'm ready to visit my old church family, for whom I've had great *saudade*.

Our old church in Nebraska has over fifty-five nations represented, from doctors to refugees, all in unity praising the Lord and storming heaven's gates in prayer. It's a taste of heaven on earth, every nation, tribe, and tongue. And in grief, there's nothing like the prayers and hugs of loved ones. Especially after such a long stint of isolation in our new town. Everywhere I sit, turn, or kneel, old friends pray over me and embrace me.

Later, as I'm weeping at the altar, right where Dan often wept, a gentleman puts his hands on my head, and I feel healing power.

What is this? This strange feeling. I kind of melt onto the stairs at the altar like a child laying her head on her mom's lap. I even smile. It's not peace coming over me because I've felt plenty of peace before in this Valley. I ask the Lord what is this unusual feeling and sense that this is called "comfort." I had not yet felt comfort.

Later, a woman kneels down and prays with me. She sends the spirit of heaviness away. She sends grief away. I've been holding on to my grief, like a way of holding on to Dan. *But, God, if it needs to go, I release it to You.*

What is this? This strange feeling. Light. Freedom. Restoration. I don't know. I can't find the right words for it. But it's as though I see the whole entire world with different eyes! I feel lighter. I see lighter. Something just lifted!

When I return to Sarita's house after intense prayer and worship,

I need another shower. In their room, I see the same thing as before. The couple holding each other and the best friend's sign. But after those prayers, instead of pain in my heart . . . *What is it?* It's like hope! It's like joy! It's like peace! Instead of devastation that I may never have that again, I'm deeply thankful I've been so richly loved. Instead of longing for what others still have, I'm so grateful that they have each other. And instead of bleak forecasts, I'm now hopeful for what's to come.

I tell Sarita all about my *what is it* moments at the altar, and we marvel. It's like Isaiah 61 was just fulfilled right in my own spirit. Jesus comforts those who mourn. And He rebuilds the former devastation. And He gives us a crown of beauty instead of ashes.

I begin to rethink everything I've ever been told about grief. What is it?

Some told me grief is a new lens I will see life through my whole life. I can see that perspective. But what if it's not? What if I can see through lenses of freedom and hope instead?

Others told me grief is my new forever friend. But, no. I don't want to befriend grief forever! Grief knocks your bones out of joint and makes your heart melt like wax.[1] What if I can befriend redemption and grace instead?

Still others speak of a season of active grief, but what comes after that? Remembering? What if that means that there's an end to the agony I felt for so long?

Sarita and I dig into root words and meanings to discover that grief has to do with afflicting pain or burden. Grief means to make heavy. And when it lifts, no wonder we feel so light again! But then what is sorrow?

In many ways, I'm back where I started . . . with lots of questions. Still not knowing exactly what grief *is*. Google doesn't know. My friends don't seem to know. I don't really know.

But one thing I've learned: sorrow is a season of becoming. And the intense agony and distressing heaviness of grief isn't intended to last forever: "the Lord will be your light forever, and the dark days of mourning will end."[2] And again it is promised, "Gladness and joy will overtake them, and sorrow and sighing will flee away."[3] In other words, the days of our sorrow will be ended. They are numbered. What good news.

───── ◆ ─────

What have you come to believe about grief these days?

Has your perspective on what grief is changed over time?

How do you feel about the thought that the days of sorrow will end? Do you hold on to your grief as a way of holding on to your person? Or can you not wait until this pain ends?

Comforter, comfort me! God of all Hope, stir up hope in me! Lift the heaviness off of me. I will wait on You and trust Your timing. But I'm asking for healing; bind my broken heart. Fill me with a sense of wonder of what You can do . . . more than I can ask or imagine! What if You really can take our mourning and turn it into dancing?[4] What if You really do rescue me because You delight in me?[5] What if I really will come out of this fire like gold?

JOHN 16:20–24 • ZEPHANIAH 3:18 • ISAIAH 60:20 • ISAIAH 35

when manna falls

Manna sustains you in the desert. But it's often unrecognizable.

God literally set the Israelites free from oppressive bondage in Egypt. He literally pushed back the seas so they could walk through to safety. They were fixing to enter the abundant harvest God had promised them. But they doubted God, trusted their fear instincts instead, and didn't go claim their victory. They were left with an extra forty years of wandering the desert. I've seen God do wonders before too, and here I am doubting He can do it again. (Oh, Father, forgive me.)

But the mystery is how God sustained them even in their desert places. He sent the sweet bread of angels[1] like rain down to earth. Israelites called the honey cakes "manna," which literally means, "What is it?"

Manna sustains you in the desert. But it's often unrecognizable.

When we hit a new rough patch in desert places, we feel like God ditched us. I thought He was giving me the cold shoulder. He wasn't. He was just showing up in a way I didn't even recognize for months and months on end. After countless desert landscapes, I slowly learned that God hadn't gone anywhere. He was just communicating in a new way; a way I didn't even perceive. *What is it?*

Manna sustains you in the desert. But it's often unrecognizable.

Sometimes I feel the Holy Spirit's presence in this peace that

I know I shouldn't naturally be able to feel when children are screaming at night or books are hurled at me in rage or the people who should be caring for us are actually stealing from us. Peace? Now? *What is it?*

It's Manna.

where can I find manna?
window, warm and sunny,
manna.
buttered bread and honey,
manna.
child, sick but snuggly,
manna.
nap for weary bones,
manna.
I am not alone.
manna.
a taste of our heavenly home—
manna.

Just reading about warm bread is comforting, isn't it? This type of poetry is called a list poem, which is simply a list with a title. List poems allow even literal, left-brained types (like my late husband) to write pretty great poetry.

I recently learned that trauma actually separates your left brain from your right brain. (That explains so much, doesn't it?) And I learned that we can work to reconnect the two hemispheres by crossing over from one side to the other. So today, I want to challenge you to use the other side of your brain. Try your hand at writing out your own list poem about ways you see Manna show up for you.

Manna falls in the form of quiet blessings and loud ones full of laughter. Let's give each piece of manna a name. A letter from a family member. A cardinal in the window. A shooting star. A meal from a friend. A gift of a haircut. A bike ride.

Now it's your turn. I'm going to walk you through the whole thing. You can fill in the blanks or you can go rogue creative. Just enjoy the process. The first four lines can be any blessings or provisions in your life right now. The last two lines can be a declaration of truth, a hope, or a prayer. Yours can rhyme. It doesn't have to.

Where Can I Find Manna?
by: _____

_____,
(a good thing in your life)
manna.

_____,
(another good thing, no matter how small)
manna.

_____,
(something else good, sustaining)
manna.

_____,
(something comforting or beautiful)
manna.

_____ ,
(a declaration of something true)
manna.

_____ ,
(any hopeful thought, request or prayer)
manna.

Ta da! You wrote your own list poem. And maybe you even crossed over from one hemisphere of your brain to the other. I'd be honored if you'd share your list poem with me:

@companioninsorrow   #whenmountainscrumble

Lord, give me eyes to see the manna that You've given me, sweet nourishment to sustain me through this season. Some days, it's hard to find even a single thing to be grateful for. On those days, help me remember something, anything. Even my breath is reason to be thankful. Help me recognize the path that You're making for me and the way You're providing for me in these desert places. You're the bread that came down from heaven to conquer death and give us life forever. For that, I thank You. In Jesus' name, amen.

JOHN 6:57–58 NLT • ISAIAH 43:18–19

when rocks cry out

My daughter's been working diligently to learn her phonograms and handwriting in kindergarten. She drew the mountains with a brown marker and sounded out some of the most powerful words I have ever read:

"Win the mowntins crombol
God has com."

When the mountains crumble, God has come. She said everything I've been trying to say throughout this whole book in seven mighty words. He has come. He is coming. He hears our SOS. He hears our cries. He sees our suffering. And He comes to our rescue.

"God is our refuge and strength,
always ready to help in times of trouble.
So we will not fear when earthquakes come
and the mountains crumble into the sea."[1]

That same evening, I found a note that my husband wrote the winter before he died. I completely forgot about it and had already drafted this entire book before I found these confirming words. I had already written about being set free in Egypt, manna from heaven, and praising God even if everything falls apart. It feels almost too sacred to share, yet I can't not. Because to God be the glory.

> I am the Lord Your God who brought you out of Egypt. I will make a way for you in the desert. The Bread of Affliction will sustain you. Even the rocks cry out in praise. Why will not my people? He who praises me in the desert places will find their rest by streams of water.

Dan wrote this down before I ever knew that I'd need a way in the desert so badly. It went on to say that God will continue writing on the hearts of man even after this book is completed. At the time, we didn't even know this book was in my future. But God did.

Surely, grief is sacred ground. Walking here is a gift we never wanted. A good gift nonetheless. Grief is drought that makes our roots press down even deeper to the living well. Grief is fertilizer that churns dirt into fertile soil. Grief surveys the scene where mountains crumble and whispers God has come, and God is with me.

Initially, we sit in the rubble and look around us, overwhelmed, shocked, and in despair. But over time, God lifts our chin and gives us naps and manna and slowly we rebuild. Just like when the Israelites sacrificed their lambs, were delivered from bondage, walked through the Red Sea, survived the desert, grieved the death of Moses, and braved entering the promised land.

Some days, we know we should be drowning, but somehow, we're walking across the raging waters on dry ground. Just like

> **Surely, grief is sacred ground. Walking here is a gift we never wanted. A good gift nonetheless.**

when God split the Red Sea and then again when He split the river Jordan.

One day, we'll gather strength to stack the broken rocks on top of each other so that when our kids ask what the stones mean, we'll tell them it's a reminder that God made a way for us because He is powerful and faithful. We declare, "Thus far the LORD has helped us."[2] What was once our faith crumbling to pieces is now rebuilt into Ebenezer stones, reminders that He got us this far, and He'll do it again. Over time, our sorrowful remembrance transforms into memories of God's faithfulness to see us through. These Ebenezer stones are landmarks of times we experienced Emmanuel, God with us.

◆

Let's take time to remember. First, draw a pile of rubble and crumbled stones at the bottom of the drawing area. Label some of these rocks with names. Maybe hopelessness, fear, anxiety, despair, insecurity . . . there are many rocks you can choose from.

Next, draw a stack of rocks that rise up on top of your rubble. Label each of these rocks with a name for different times you saw God's help, provision, goodness, or mercy. Maybe names of people who helped you, unique ways you noticed God reminding you He cares, bittersweet blessings, and manna in the desert.

@companioninsorrow   #whenmountainscrumble

That's a powerful image right there. May your drawing help you (and generations after you) to remember that the Lord got you this far and He will help you finish your journey. Return to your drawing and to the following liturgy whenever you feel like your world is falling apart. May they help you find your footing again:

A Liturgy for When Mountains Crumble
When our faith crumbles,
God has come.
When our dreams die,
God has come.
When everything falls apart,
God has come.
God has come, He is coming,
and He will come again.

God, You are my Rock and my salvation.
When I thought I would drown, You dried up the path to safe ground. I stack rocks as a reminder to me and others that my God is powerful and faithful. You got me this far. I trust You'll do it again. In Jesus' name, amen.

ISAIAH 7:14 • ISAIAH 9:6 • PSALM 23 • JOSHUA 4:19–24

when eagles fly

My oldest fell and sprained an ankle our first autumn without Dan. The season when everything kept breaking. But now, she's feeling courageous and the sunshine beckons us out of our wintering indoors.

My youngest was ready to ride her bike without training wheels before we moved here, but after big changes like a move or a tragedy, we regress. Regression is a natural part of the process of moving forward.

We learned about regression two duty stations prior when my oldest daughter learned to ride her bike right before we moved to Nebraska and the change set her back. New streets. New hills. New neighbors. She had just said goodbye to everyone she knew and loved in Florida: dolphins, best friends, and grandma types. It was too much. So we put the training wheels back on her bike until she felt more stable and secure in the new environment.

The body regresses sometimes to give the heart as much attention and energy as possible. That's why young children often begin sucking their thumbs or wetting the bed or baby talk after a big change, move, or loss. Processing loss is demanding on the mind and soul, so if we step back developmentally, we save energy to work on the shock of what just happened.

Loss does that to adults too. It sets us back. I've pitched bigger tantrums than my two-year-old children since losing Dan.

Regression's not permanent. We'll ride without training wheels again. But in loss, we sometimes need to give ourselves the grace to put the training wheels back on.

I went back to a gluten-free, dairy-free diet. Even though God did a miracle just months prior to Dan's death and healed me of all my food allergies. But after losing Dan, I had to let my body regress and give it less work. I had to stop folding laundry every day. I had to use the training wheels of paper plates. I'm okay with that.

My training wheels looked like getting to school late almost every day and not worrying about academics. Getting there at all was a victory. Training wheels still look like lots of mental health days in pajamas, for me and my children.

We naturally hang on to our crutches as long as possible. Because we get used to them. In them, we've taken comfort. But then the day comes when the wheels come off. Today, I asked my youngest (who has been ready for a long time!) if she was ready to take off her training wheels. I felt a low-level anxiety leading up to this day. Because of course, I wish Daddy could be here to run with her and cheer her on and let her rip. But it's me and sister. And I'm a witness that their childhood is still joyful.

So, with some low-level anxiety and a big dose of missing Dan, I figured out the wrench situation and took off the training wheels. I helped get her started and held her balance for less than three seconds. And she was off!

She flew! Steady. Stable. Soaring. *She flew!* We sat back, cheered, and celebrated. We're alive! We are in the land of the living, and we will see goodness and mercy here.[1] Grief is sacred ground, even if we walk it with crutches or ride it with training wheels. I trust that there will be a day when our training wheels will come off and once again, you and I will fly too.

"Even youths will become weak and tired,
and young men will fall in exhaustion.
But those who trust in the LORD will find new strength.
They will soar high on wings like eagles.
They will run and not grow weary.
They will walk and not faint."[2]

In other words, those who trust in the Lord, they'll fly when they should be falling!

I couldn't help but picture Daddy on one side of her and our Father in Heaven on her other side, running beside her. Because our God, He also knows what it's like to lose someone He loves, His very own Son. And Jesus knows what it's like to grieve. He gave up everything to be able to be near to us, the brokenhearted. He trades us beauty for our ashes, our mourning for His joy. And He'll always be by our side. He is our closest companion in sorrow. He is our joy in the morning. He walks us through the valley. And He teaches us to soar on wings like eagles.

As my oldest and I jump up and down and celebrate, I remember the months she could not jump, walk, or cheer. We prayed three times that night for healing for her sprained ankle, asking her to see how it feels after each time. It was scary for her, to think about walking without the crutches. It usually is. That's why Jesus first asks us, "Do you want to be healed?"

Sometimes, we don't want to. We're not ready. We want the training wheels and the crutches longer than we need. But with courage and great faith, she took baby steps putting weight on her ankle. By the end, she was running in the sanctuary. *Running!* We all grow tired and weary, even youth, but those who trust in the Lord will fly and not fall, will run and not faint. They will ride bikes without training wheels and will run without crutches.

The three of us ride our bikes around the loop, over and over together. We could not smile wider. This is a victory for us all with deep roots. When we take a break, the girls collect intricate tiny purple flowers and little buds of yellow ones too. I will call the purple ones "peace" and the yellow ones "joy!" wrapping my arms around my little girls, beaming. The sun, much bigger than I, embraces us all. And I know. We're going to be okay. We're going to make it.

◆

What do your training wheels look like in this season?

Have you seen some training wheels come off already? What steps toward healing have you made?

Trace and retrace these words as many times as you need to:

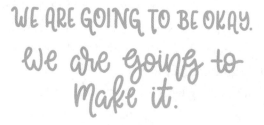

God of all hope, thank You for drawing near to the
brokenhearted instead of avoiding us. Thank You
for being full of mercy for our mess-ups instead of
condemning us. Thank You for cheering on the sidelined
and welcoming the outcast. Thank You for being a
Father to the fatherless, a defender of the widow. Fill us
with joy and peace as we trust in You, that we may be
overflowing in hope by the power of the Holy Spirit.[3]

ROMANS 15:13 • ISAIAH 54:10 • ISAIAH 61

God is our refuge and strength,
an ever-present help in trouble.
Therefore we will not fear, though the earth give way
and the mountains fall into the heart of the sea,
though its waters roar and foam
and the mountains quake with their surging.
There is a river whose streams make glad the city of God,
the holy place where the Most High dwells.
God is within her, she will not fall;
God will help her at break of day.
Nations are in uproar, kingdoms fall;
he lifts his voice, the earth melts.
The LORD Almighty is with us;
the God of Jacob is our fortress.
Come and see what the LORD has done,
the desolations he has brought on the earth.
He makes wars cease
to the ends of the earth.
He breaks the bow and shatters the spear;
he burns the shields with fire.
He says, "Be still, and know that I am God;
I will be exalted among the nations,
I will be exalted in the earth."
The LORD Almighty is with us;
the God of Jacob is our fortress.

PSALM 46

Additional Resources

I'm humbled that you've allowed me to be part of your grief journey. And I'd love to stay in touch.

If you haven't already, join me at **companioninsorrow.com** where you'll find:

- Your Grief Guide (full of practical ideas and a quick orientation)

- Your Scripture Sidekick (every Scripture referenced in this book)

- Printable Prayers for Healing and Freedom

- Original Printable Artwork

- The Companion in Sorrow Playlist

- My Favorite Movies of Sorrow Watchlist

- Grief Relief Recipes

- Resources for Coping and Sleep

- Links to Grief Support Groups

- If you're here to help a grieving friend and want to learn how to walk with them through grief, visit **companioninsorrow. com** to download the Companion's Grief Guide. This is full of practical ways to help, including how to know what to say and not to say, what you need to know to support them well, a sympathy card download, gift ideas, etc.

I pray you find your footing for your next steps moving forward and that you find continual signs of redemption when looking back. Thank you for walking this long, hard road with me.

♡Hanita jenae

Many Thanks

Lord, thank You for Your Unshakable Love. Thank You for Your quiet presence and Your soothing Words. Thank You for weeping with me instead of avoiding me. Thank You for embracing me when I'm lashing out. Thank You for being a God who draws near to the brokenhearted. Thank You that You seek out those who are crushed in spirit. Thank You that You are the Lifter of my head when it hangs low in sorrow.

Father, please pass this on to Dan, my love: Thank you for loving me like Christ loves the Church, with such undeserved and lavish kindness. Thank you for loving me and the girls with everything in you—through forgiveness, fasting, prayers, weeping, dancing, laughter, adventure, mercy. Everything in me aches for you. Your smile is unforgettable. You were everything I prayed for in a husband, and my list was long and deep. Thank you for your blessing over me, our girls, and our future. Thank you for your legacy of prayer. It has sustained me, knowing God continues to answer the prayers you stored up for me and our children and loved ones. I love you.

Thank you, my beautiful children who overflow with peace and joy. There is so much of your daddy's servant-hearted leadership and ever-loving kindness in you. Thank you for giving Mama abundant encouragement, forgiveness, grace, and hope for the future. Thank you for dancing with me in the living room, even so. Thank you for the gift of sharing your laughter and the sacred ground of your tears with me. I love you with my whole heart.

Thank you, Mom and Dad, for giving us a safe place to fall. Thank you for your extraordinary generosity and servants' hearts. And thanks for taking us to funerals as kids. It taught us that funerals are a normal, healthy part of life. Thank you for showing me that God hears our prayers. Thank you for praying for my husband, decades before we got to meet him. I love you, to Jesus' house and back.

Thank you, Mammy and Papa, for adopting us and loving us as your own. Thank you for your prayers, help, and warm welcome as part of the family. Thank you for praying for Dan's bride when he was a kid, since before I was even born. I love you dearly.

Thank you, HeeMa, for showing me that joy and sorrow can go together; it gives me hope. I think of HeePa all the time. *Hark!* I love you always and forever. Thank you to Granddaddy and Grandma for your tears; they mean the world. I've watched your courage to make the calls to let others know about people we've loved and lost so many times. I love you forever and always.

Thank you for being there for me, brothers and sisters, and our "whole flamily." It's so good to be loved by you. I love y'all so much.

Thank you, beloved prayer warriors. We've seen clouds pushed back, sickness healed, doors opened, and heaviness lifted. Where would I be without you? Thank you for those I've never met who prayed for us and still do. Your prayers helped us walk on water.

Thank you to my guides, leads, walking partners, porters, fellow stragglers, sweepers, and cheering team of family, friends, church family, military, and neighbors. I'm so grateful for every time you showed up at just the right time like angels with hot bread. Thank you, my companions in sorrow who got me through those most isolating months. Thank you, beloved heavy-lifters, broken-things-fixers, book-launchers, snow-shovelers, horse-gentlers, hand-holders, pre-readers, mouth-feeders, gift-givers, and babysitters. Partnering with God, you've made things that were impossible for us possible.

Thank you pastors, prayer mentors, prayer teams, Bible study leaders, deliverance teams, prophetic teams, and care teams from all the beautiful churches we've been part of over the years. You got me this far. Thank you for raising me and fighting for me in the spirit.

Thank you to my English teachers. You gave me the gift of writing, a gift that saved my life many times. And you made me believe I was an author decades before I was one.

Thank you Ms. Blythe, Ms. Judy, Ms. Amanda, and the entire Moody Publishers team. Thank you Julia Deese for letting us include your beautiful handwritten calligraphy. And thank you Laurie for putting the Scripture Sidekick together. You've all fought for me, shown me great kindness, and protected my heart in this. Thank you for your patience with me as I navigated this new terrain without Dan by my side.

It's funny. Grief makes you feel so very alone, but the truth is I have been so very loved. If I could list you all by name, you'd fill this book! But I thank God for you by name in my prayers. Mostly, I thank God that each of your names is written in the Lamb's Book of Life. For each of you, I pray God pours out His quiet blessings and loud ones full of laughter.

Notes

1. Luke 4:21 ERV.

My Story and the Sangre de Cristo Mountains
1. John 11:35.
2. Revelation 12:11.

Grief 101
1. Andy McNeil, "Connecting and Communicating with Your Grieving Child or Teenager," *Southern Regional Virtual Military Survivor Seminar,* February 28, 2021, Dallas: TAPS Institute for Hope and Healing, https://www.taps.org/seminars/2021/southern#child.
2. C. S. Lewis, *A Grief Observed* (San Francisco: HarperOne, 2001).

misplacing wednesdays (grief brain)
1. Ralph Waldo Emerson, selected and ed. by Joel Porte, *Emerson in His Journals* (Cambridge, MA: The Belknap Press of Harvard University Press, 1982), 277.

where can i hide? (grief covering)
1. Exodus 12:27.
2. Exodus 12:23.
3. Exodus 12:7–12; 11:6.
4. Ephesians 1:4–6, TLB.

i can't move (grief fever)
1. Randi Maples, "Peer Support Services: PTS Treatment for the Surviving Spouse," *Angels of America's Fallen and KAB Medical,* Virtual Seminar, October 17, 2020.
2. Previously posted on author's Instagram, @danitajenae, November 14, 2019.
3. Ephesians 5:14.

moving forward (grief courage)
1. Matthew 6:33.

who am i anymore? (grief + identity)
1. Hebrews 12:27 NLT.
2. Isaiah 54:10.

mapping sorrow
1. Eric Weiner, Chris Gifford, and Valerie Walsh, *Dora the Explorer,* Nickelodeon Animation Studio, 2000–2019.
2. Isaiah 43:15–19.

the faulty five stages
1. Elisabeth Kübler-Ross, *On Death and Dying: What the Dying Have to Teach Doctors, Nurses, Clergy & Their Own Families* (New York: Scribner, 1969).
2. David B. Feldman, "Why the Five Stages of Grief Are Wrong: Lessons from the (Non-) Stages of Grief," *Psychology Today*, July 7, 2017, https://www.psychology today.com/us/blog/supersurvivors/201707/why-the-five-stages-grief-are-wrong.
3. Allan Kellehear, "Dr. Elisabeth Kübler-Ross and the Five Stages of Grief," EKR Foundation, https://www.ekrfoundation.org/5-stages-of-grief/5-stages-grief/. Excerpt on website is taken from Dr. Allan Kellehear's introduction in Elisabeth Kübler-Ross's *On Death and Dying: What the Dying Have to Teach Doctors, Nurses, Clergy and Their Own Families*, 40th Anniversary Edition (London: Routledge, 2009).
4. Margaret Stroebe, Henk Schut, and Kathrin Boerner, "Cautioning Health-Care Professionals: Bereaved Persons Are Misguided through Stages of Grief," *OMEGA- Journal of Death and Dying* 74, no. 4 (2017): 455–73, https://doi .org/10.1177%2F0030222817691870.
5. Marian Osterweis, Fredric Solomon, and Morris Green, *Bereavement: Reactions, Consequences, and Care* (Washington, DC: National Academy Press, 1984), 48.
6. Roxane Cohen Silver and Camille B. Wortman. "The Stage Theory of Grief," *The Journal of the American Medical Association* 297, no. 24 (2007): 2692, https://doi .org/10.1001/jama.297.24.2692-a.
7. Feldman, "Why the Five Stages of Grief Are Wrong: Lessons from the (Non-) Stages of Grief."
8. Elisabeth Kübler-Ross and David Kessler, *On Grief & Grieving: Finding the Meaning of Grief through the Five Stages of Loss* (New York: Scribner, 2014), 7.

sippy cups and avoidance
1. Matthew 5:4.

feast or famine
1. Psalm 34:9–10.
2. Psalm 18:19.

switchbacks and setbacks
1. Quote by John Rutledge on author's blog with permission, "They Say, 'Time Heals All Wounds.' But It Doesn't," danitajenae.com, March 25, 2020, https://danitajenae .com/they-say-time-heals-all-wounds-but-it-doesnt/.
2. Previously posted on author's site, danitajenae.com, March 25, 2020, https://dani tajenae.com/they-say-time-heals-all-wounds-but-it-doesnt/.

life-giving list
1. Holmes-Rahe Stress Inventory, The American Institute of Stress, https://www .stress.org/holmes-rahe-stress-inventory.
2. 2 Corinthians 10:5.

horses and healing
1. Acts 17:28.

blessings, bittersweet
1. 1 Corinthians 15:55.
2. 2 Corinthians 4:17–18.

when they pass the baton
1. A song the author learned in Girl Scouts. The original song was written by Joseph Parry in the 1800s.

when they say dumb things
1. Matthew 6:10.
2. Matthew 18:22, KJV.

build a prayer team
1. Matthew 18:20, NKJV.
2. Numbers 6:22–27.

when they ask how you're doing
1. Psalm 34:9.

permission to ask why
1. Jeff Arch, Nora Ephron, and David S. Ward, *Sleepless in Seattle,* directed by Nora Ephron, Tri-Star Pictures, 1993.
2. Matthew 27:46.
3. Matthew 27:45–26.
4. Mark 9:24.

surrendering whys
1. Galatians 5:1.
2. John 10:10.
3. Romans 15:13.
4. Elisabeth Elliot, *On Asking God Why: Reflections on Trusting God* (Grand Rapids: Revell, 1989), 18.

flipping whys
1. Graham Cooke, *Radical Perceptions: Brilliant Thoughts For an Amazing Life* (Vacaville, CA: Brilliant Book House, 2011), chapter 4, n.p.
2. Ibid.
3. Ibid.

Jesus asking why
1. Luke 23:46.
2. Mark 15:34.
3. James 2:13.
4. Genesis 50:20.
5. Luke 23:34.
6. Hebrews 12:2.
7. Galatians 2:20.
8. Genesis 50:20.

blaming God for why
1. Daniel 3:17.
2. Daniel 3:18.
3. Revelation 19:11–13.

the ministry of lament
1. Proverbs 24:26.
2. John 6:68–69.
3. Job 13:15.
4. Jonah 4:8.
5. Luke 22:44.
6. Adapted from author's blog: "The Intersection Between Faith and Feelings," October 2, 2019, https://danitajenae.com/the-intersection-between-faith-and-feelings/.

the ministry of tears
1. Emily P. Freeman, opening session, the Hope*Writer Conference, Charlotte, North Carolina, November 6, 2019.
2. Hebrews 5:7.
3. Romans 8:26, ESV.
4. Revelation 7:17.
5. Psalm 56:8, NKJV.

when you want to give up
1. 1 Kings 19.

the ministry of smoke alarms
1. Lysa TerKeurst, *Unglued: Making Wise Choices in the Midst of Raw Emotions* (Nashville: Nelson Books, 2012), 72.
2. Psalm 37:8.

the what ifs
1. 1 John 1:7.
2. Quin Sherrer, *Hope for a Widow's Heart: Encouraging Reflections For Your Journey* (Franklin: Authentic Publishers, 2013), 27.
3. 1 Peter 5:8.
4. 2 Chronicles 16:9.
5. John 10:10.
6. Philippians 4:6–7.
7. Matthew 11:29.
8. Hebrews 4:15.
9. Romans 8:1.

the coulda-woulda-shouldas
1. Isaiah 26:3, Romans 15:13.
2. Psalm 121:1–2.
3. Judson W. Van DeVenter, "I Surrender All," 1896, Public Domain.
4. Matthew 23:3.
5. Zephaniah 3:17.
6. Adapted from the author's blog: "Shooting Stars at the Trailhead: On Loss and Grief and Mysteries," August 23, 2019, https://danitajenae.com/shooting-stars-at-the-trailhead-on-loss-grief-and-mysteries/.
7. Proverbs 3:3–5.

the veil between heaven and earth
1. Luke 23:32–49.
2. Joel 2:32, Romans 10:13.

3. Isaiah 8:19.
4. Ephesians 3:20.
5. Jeremiah 33:3.

the legacy of prayer
1. James 5:16.
2. Proverbs 11:21, KJV.
3. Mark Batterson, *Draw the Circle: The 40 Day Prayer Challenge* (Grand Rapids: Zondervan, 2012), 203.

when it hits the fan
1. Genesis 50:20.
2. Ephesians 4:29.
3. Proverbs 18:21, KJV.
4. Romans 8:28, Genesis 50:20.
5. Lamentations 3:22–23.

when the Holy Spirit takes the wheel
1. Psalm 22:14.
2. Isaiah 60:20, ERV.
3. Isaiah 35:10.
4. Psalm 30:11, NKJV.
5. Psalm 18:19, ESV.

when manna falls
1. Psalm 78:25.

when rocks cry out
1. Psalm 46:1–2, NLT.
2. 1 Samuel 7:12.

when eagles fly
1. Psalm 27:13.
2. Isaiah 40:30–31, NLT.
3. Romans 15:13.

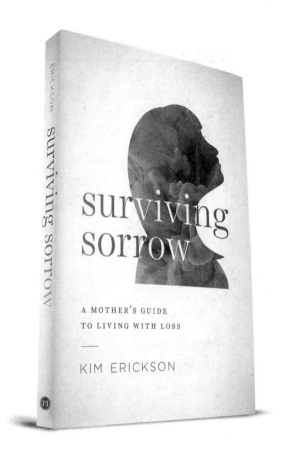

SUFFERING IS A SEASON.
HOPE IS ETERNAL.

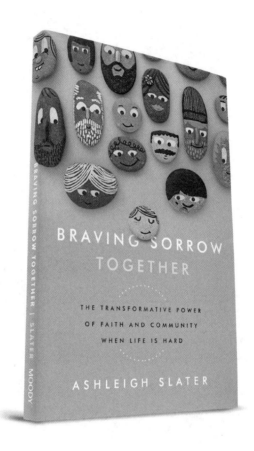

Braving Sorrow Together examines the nature of grief and loss in several universal arenas such as relationships, health, career, and the home. For anyone who ever struggles—and that's all of us—*Braving Sorrow Together* teaches how to move through trials with wisdom, releasing anxiety, and receiving the help and comfort God so bountifully provides.

978-0-8024-1659-9 | also available as eBook and audiobook

Can joy come from suffering?

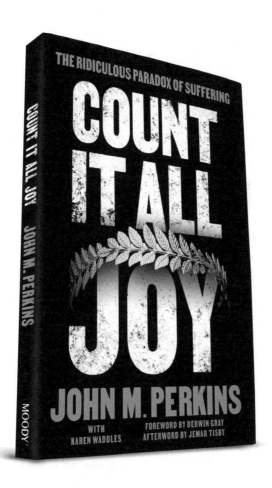